TRAMWAYS REMEMBERED

East Anglia, East Midlands & Lincolnshire

Leslie Oppitz

D1471380

COUNTRYSIDE BOOKS

NEWBURY, BERKSHIRE

Also by Leslie Oppitz
Tramways Remembered – West & South West England
Tramways Remembered – South & South East England
Chilterns Railways Remembered
Dorset Railways Remembered
East Anglia Railways Remembered
Hereford & Worcester Railways Remembered
Sussex Railways Remembered
Surrey Railways Remembered
Kent Railways Remembered
Hampshire Railways Remembered
(with Kevin Robertson)

TO DAVID CLAYRE
Another Dedicated Tramway Enthusiast

Cover picture shows Leicester's tramcar no 76, originally built in 1904 as an open-top car. The car is currently on display at the National Tramway Museum at Crich, where members have converted it back to its 1920 condition. (Picture by kind permission of The National Tramway Museum, Crich)

First Published 1992
© Leslie Oppitz 1992

COUNTRYSIDE BOOKS
3 Catherine Road
Newbury Berkshire

ISBN 1 85306 132 8

Produced through MRM Associates Ltd., Reading
Typeset by Acorn Bookwork, Salisbury
Printed in England

Contents

York
Hull
Immingham
Grimsby
Cleethorpes
Sheffield
Sutton-on-Sea
Alford
Lincoln
Boston
Skegness
Cromer
Derby
Nottingham
King's Lynn
Great
Yarmouth
Leicester
Wisbech
Norwich
Upwell
Lowestoft
Birmingham
Peterborough
Carlton
Colville
Coventry
Northampton
Cambridge
Stony
Stratford
Bedford
Ipswich
Wolverton
Felixstowe
Luton
Colchester
Harwich
Walton-on-the-Naze
Oxford
Chelmsford
Canvey
Island
Southend-on-Sea
London
Croydon
Folkestone
Dover

Brian Butler '91

Key:

Principal Tram Towns
and Pier Tramways
as featured in book

ACKNOWLEDGEMENTS

Acknowledgements go to the numerous libraries, record offices and museums throughout the Eastern Counties and many of the surrounding areas, where staff have delved into records. Thanks go to John H. Meredith, also J L Smith of Lens of Sutton for their help in the supply of many early pictures.

Thanks also go to the following who generously contributed with information:

Desmond Adams and Nicholas Kelly, fellow enthusiasts; Peggy Dowie, chairman of the Southend Pier Museum Foundation; J H Price MCIT, of Peterborough; George Gundry of Wimbledon SW 19; Roger Benton, The National Tramway Museum, Crich; C W Sampson, Director General Manager and Engineer, Colchester Borough Transport Ltd; Stephen Cobb, Secretary, Ipswich Transport Museum; Steve Worsley of Ipswich; John Preston, Hon Secretary, East Anglia Transport Museum, Carlton Colville; John Renton, Assistant Keeper of Social History, The Bridewell Museum, Norwich; Stanley R Taylor, ex-City Mace Bearer, Guildhall, Norwich; Mrs Joan Doy, Administrator, Milton Keynes Museum of Industry and Rural Life, Wolverton; Mrs Zoe Pagis, Alford Manor House Museum, Alford, Lincolnshire; John Horrocks, Director of Engineering & Supplies, Northampton Transport; Peter M Smith, Llandudno & Colwyn Bay Electric Railway Society; Roy Waterton, Superintendent, Stockwood Craft Museum, Luton; Mark Pearson, Author of 'Leicester's Trams in Retrospect'; R Bracegirdle, Curator of Science and Industry, Industrial Heritage Project, Coalville, Leicester; A P Jarram, Brush Transport Enthusiasts' Club; Mike Dobson of Lincoln.

Personal thanks go to Colin Withey, a dedicated transport enthusiast for loaning further old pictures, as well as spending much time carefully checking the final manuscript, Brian Butler for preparing the maps and to my wife, Joan, for travelling the many counties with me and also proving herself once again an able proof-reader.

INTRODUCTION

Passengers climb aboard an open-top double-deck Lowestoft tram and take their seats in the saloon – the driver sounds his gong – and the vehicle pulls slowly away. The car, built by Milnes in 1904, seats 22 in the saloon and another 26 'on top'. A conductor punches tickets and the tram makes its way along a cobbled street, past a cafe and various shops to its first stop. The scene might well have been a street in Lowestoft around the 1920s, but it happened in fact in 1990! The car was one of many superbly restored by the members of the East Anglia Transport Museum at Carlton Colville which can be found just off the Beccles – Lowestoft (A146) road.

Trams originated in New York in 1832 where in the United States today they are still referred to as 'streetcars'. There had been great enthusiasm as two horse-drawn single-deck cars reached 'breathtaking' speeds on the flat iron strips that served as rails. In 1860 trams reached Birkenhead, introduced to this country by an American called (inappropriately) George Francis Train. The system, just over 1¼ miles in length, opened on August 30th with the claim that it was the 'first street tramway in Europe'.

London saw its first trams in March 1861 when Train laid tracks between Marble Arch and Notting Hill Gate, with the first car pulled by two horses. Two other routes followed, one from Westminster to Victoria Station and another from Westminster Bridge to Kennington Park. George Train considered his tramcars a transport for the wealthy although history has shown that the reverse became true.

These early systems proved popular enough but they failed in London because the wrong type of track had been chosen. A step rail was used, an L-shaped rail with a vertical section protruding above the road surface, and this became unpopular with other road users. Many horse-drawn carriages had their wheels ripped off when crossing at an angle so the lines where forced to close within a year. On the 1860 line in Birkenhead, events transpired differently since the track was eventually replaced by an improved cross-section rail.

One of the first undertakings in England's Eastern Counties came about in October 1880 when a horse tramway system began services in the city of Cambridge. In 1883 steam trams began services between Wisbech and Upwell primarily to assist agriculture in the area. Within a short time they were carrying some 3,000 passengers each week in addition to around 600 tons of goods. Another rural steam tramway followed the next year when services opened between Alford and Sutton-on-Sea in Lincolnshire.

When electric trams were introduced in Norwich in July 1900, they proved immediately popular and it was not long before many other towns followed with their own systems. When trams came to Southend-on-Sea in July 1901, grandiose ideas followed for light railways to link Southend with places such as Burnham-on-Crouch and even Colchester. But the ideas came to nothing. Such proposals generally received strong opposition from the main railway companies and there was usually insufficient financial support.

Once installed, the towns put their trams to good use. In times when most people walked because money was short, the new transport provided a new – and cheap – method of travel where previously it might not have been possible. Further electric undertakings were soon to follow. Later in 1901, trams linked Grimsby with Cleethorpes and in 1902 services started at Great Yarmouth, eventually to reach Caister-on-Sea to the north and Gorlestone-on-Sea to the south. During 1903, further systems opened at Peterborough, Lowestoft and Ipswich with many others following over the next year or so. Alas, plans to join the Great Yarmouth and Lowestoft systems came to nothing.

This book provides a comprehensive coverage of the lives of these tramways throughout the Eastern Counties of England, from the river Thames to the river Humber, bordered on the western side for much of the area by the M1 motorway. In addition, there are recollections of one of the largest British tramcar manufacturers – Brush at Loughborough. The book also enables the reader to explore for himself throughout the region the many relics that have survived the years. Looking to the future, there are exciting times ahead as trams make a comeback. The congested town centres in many areas today make it imperative for an alternative transport system to be introduced. Numerous Rapid Transit Systems are already under active review and these receive due consideration.

Chapter 1

TRAMS ALONG THE ESTUARY

(Southend-on-Sea Corporation Light Railways, Southend-on-Sea
Cliff Railway and the Electric Tram That Came (to Canvey) and
Didn't Stop)

Southend-on-Sea Corporation Light Railways
When Southend's trams began their first day of public operation,
there were numerous problems. Many of the staff had received
only a week of training and it was not surprising that at passing
loops numerous trolley arms became detached from the overhead
wires. There were also breakdowns and minor collisions. To make
matters worse there were occasional failures in current supply from
the power station.

The system was formally opened on 19th July 1901 by local
dignitaries with passenger services commencing immediately. Fortunately there were no serious accidents on the first day and, with
the holiday season beginning, the difficulties proved more a novelty
to the crowds than a problem. Many of those present were
Londoners on holiday and it was the first time for most of them
that they had seen an electric tram. Consequently traffic was heavy
and every available car was in use. Even the lack of route indicators
on the cars failed to dampen any spirits with the conductor having
to shout out the destination at each stop.

In the early part of the 19th century Southend was a small village
in the southern part of the parish of Prittlewell referred to as the
'south end'. There had been attempts to rival Brighton as a
'watering place' but the lack of travel facilities had made this
difficult. Approach along the river Thames was also a problem due
to the large mud flats off the coast. It was for these reasons that
Royal Assent was given in 1829 to the building of a pier. When

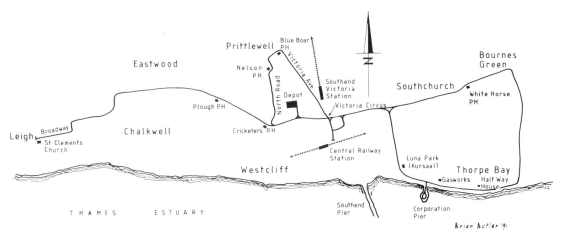

Southend — on — Sea   Corporation   Light   Railways

completed in 1846 it was of necessity one and a quarter miles long with a single track tramway built along its length. (The story of Southend's pier is given in the next chapter.) When the London, Tilbury & Southend Railway came in 1856, the area quickly developed as a resort with many trippers coming to the town.

By the time the Great Eastern Railway reached the area in 1889, the population had grown to around 12,000. The following year the Borough of Southend came into being and in 1893 the town changed its name to Southend-on-Sea. The number of trippers, particularly from East London, continued to increase with the area becoming known to many as 'the Cockney's paradise'. It was becoming evident that, in addition to the pier tramway, some form of transport was needed through the town.

First ideas for a tramway came in 1883/4 when a line was proposed from Southend via Rochford to the ferry to Burnham-on-Crouch. This did not materialise but when the corporation extended its seafront in 1897 numerous companies approached the borough for support for the construction of an electric tramway. Since the corporation was about to launch an electric lighting scheme, it was felt that local interests could best be served by promoting a tramway itself. Taking advantage of The Light Railways Act passed the year previously, the corporation applied for a Light Railway Order to build a town tramway system with an option to follow up with interurban extensions at a later date.

Accordingly in July 1898 proposals were put forward for routes across the town from Leigh to Southchurch and from Prittlewell to the seafront. Further lines had been proposed through Westcliff but when the local residents heard of this, the idea was fiercely contested and was withdrawn. In addition a proposed route along Pier Hill and Marine Parade was dropped because of finance and the technical difficulties in coping with the steep road. Work went ahead in February 1900 on a 3 ft 6 ins gauge tramway with an overhead wire current collection system.

At first a total track length of 6¼ miles was envisaged with much of it being built along country roads. A depot was provided not far

Crossbench car no 41 on a 'circular tour' along Southchurch Boulevard. Sensible planning in the earlier times kept the tramcars away from the roads on preserved tracks. (Lens of Sutton)

from Victoria Circus in the London Road. Construction included a route from The Middleton Hotel by Central station to Prittlewell and back to the Cricketers, a line from Southchurch to Eastwood and Leigh and another via Southchurch Road to the Minerva Hotel. Unfortunately work proceeded slower than expected due to delays in placing sub-contracts and because of the unexpected gravelly nature of the subsoil. When little progress had been made at the end of 1900, the corporation insisted that one section should be completed so that drivers could be trained. This the contractor refused to do so the corporation warned that if the whole system was not completed by Easter 1901, then legal action would be taken.

Meantime 14 cars were ordered from the Brush Electrical & Engineering Co Ltd. These included two single-deck cars each with 20 seats, ten open top cars each with 38 seats and two open top cars fitted with bogies each with 58 seats. Two each of these arrived in March with the intention that driver instruction could commence but when Easter came the contractor said that a further three months' work was necessary. As threatened, the corporation took legal action for non-fulfilment of contract and loss of earnings. Eventually on 10th July 1901 the Board of Trade inspectors passed the lines (except for a short section not completed in Corporation Avenue) as satisfactory and public service began one week later.

The tramcars' basic colours were two contrasting shades of green and advertisements were carried on the 'decency boards' on the upper deck and the end screens. Longitudinal wooden seats were provided in the saloon overlaid with carpet. On top, the seating was transverse with double one side and single the other. Lighting upstairs came from a lantern fitted to a pedestal at each end. There were initially no route indicator boards.

In June 1901, a company known as the Railways & General Construction & Maintenance Co Ltd announced plans to build a 4 ft 8½ in gauge light railway line from Southend to Burnham-on-Crouch and on to Bradwell-on-Sea. Since the southern end was in

11

the Borough of Southend's area, the corporation opposed the idea strongly. In November 1901 the company made a further attempt, but this time for a Light Railway Order from Southend to Colchester. Again the Borough of Southend stated its opposition yet at the same time declared an interest in constructing itself a section of the line, from Prittlewell to Rochford, yet this was not to come about. At a hearing, the proposal to reach Colchester was turned down as impractical although some years of planning activity continued with the scheme last heard of in 1925.

Southend's trams proved popular although this was largely through holiday traffic. The open top single truck cars were found to be inadequate for the summer traffic and in April 1902 three new bogie cars were supplied. These were the first cars to carry any indicator boards thus helping to avoid the frequent confusion caused at the High Street terminus. The two single deck cars were used on the Prittlewell route where traffic was disappointingly light. Since it was only a short distance, intending passengers often chose to walk, finding this quicker.

Revenue remained disappointing, partly because there were insufficient cars so a further five were ordered for delivery in May 1904. These were built by Milnes mounted on Brill trucks each equipped with two 25 hp motors and capable of seating 64 passengers. Also during 1904 efforts were made to expand the system, Bryant Avenue on the Eastern Esplanade being reached by 1908. Agreement was given to proceed with lines to Bournes Green and Shoeburyness. The latter proposal did not go ahead and instead, after many years of delay and indecision, a 1¾ mile tramway was built in 1913–1914 between Southchurch and Thorpe Bay, via Bournes Green, on reserved track thus providing a circular route. These boulevard tracks to the east of the town became a show place of colour from the thousands of shrubs and trees planted by the corporation. This tram route soon became the subject of many colourful postcards that were sent to friends extolling the pleasures of a day at Southend.

The fleet now comprised some 38 cars with the two original single deck cars having been rebuilt in 1907–1908 as double deck cars each seating 44 passengers. Others had been lengthened to accommodate extra passengers and a number were rebuilt with canopies. With the new 'boulevard' extension available, three single deck crossbench 'toast rack' trams were purchased. Holiday-makers were able to enjoy circular tours which imitated the good revenue earners of Blackpool and Southport. The tours started and finished on the front at the Kursaal with no intermediate stops, providing passengers with delightful views along the estuary before turning the corner at Thorpe Bay to the colour of the boulevards. A charge of 6d (2½p) was made for adults and 3d (just over 1p) for children.

When war came in 1914 services were considerably reduced as many holidaymakers made for home. When German Zeppelin raids began in January 1915, all coastal towns had to take complete blackout precautions. With the Germans using the course of the Thames to reach London, Southend became particularly vulnerable. At first cars ran with no lights at all but later dim internal illumination was permitted. In addition tram headlamps were coated with white paint to reduce their beam. Destination indicator boards remained unlit so as to confuse the enemy!

In February 1915 components arrived to equip three wagons so that coal, arriving by sea to the Corporation Pier coal jetty, could be delivered to the municipal power station. A circular tram track had been constructed on the pier, located off Southchurch Beach Road not far from the Kursaal. The wagons had a roofed driving cab at each end with a trolley mast between two hoppers. These wagons remained in service until 1929 when supplies were taken from the national grid.

Toast-Rack trams at the depot off the London Road which were popular on the circular route from the Kursaal along the Boulevards. (Lens of Sutton)

Meantime the trams remained busy despite the war. With many troops stationed at Shoeburyness Garrison, a service to Thorpe Bay was much in demand and it was considered unfortunate that earlier plans to extend the tramway to the town had not materialised. Using Thorpe Bay as a terminus gave problems. It became necessary to leave ropes permanently attached to the trolley poles of the open top cars being the only means they could be turned. On dark nights this often proved difficult with the overhead wire almost invisible, a problem also experienced at the High Street terminus. The situation was hazardous too for unsuspecting passengers moving about on the upper deck who occasionally received a hefty clout from the trolley arm being pulled too low.

As the war progressed, the system suffered not only from lack of maintenance but also from shortage of skilled personnel. In 1916 women were recruited as conductresses and the three open cross bench 'toast rack' cars were temporarily converted to more practical use as saloons by fixing panelling and windows to the sides. The benches were turned round to form longitudinal seating down each side. Despite the problems of the war, the system struggled on. In 1917 the section from 'Nelson Hotel', Prittlewell, to the 'Cricketers Hotel' at Leigh was abandoned. In July 1918 trolley reversers were installed at the termini to ease trolley turning in the blackout just months before the war was over!

During the early 1920s further cars were ordered and the three cross bench cars were converted back to their original use. In September 1925 the town saw its first trolleybus with another following the next month. Both vehicles were used to supplement the trams on the Prittlewell route. The track on this section had never been relaid and was in a very poor state, so early in 1926 temporary repairs were put in hand. On 3rd April all services stopped due to the General Strike and it was only thanks to the

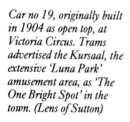

Car no 19, originally built in 1904 as open top, at Victoria Circus. Trams advertised the Kursaal, the extensive 'Luna Park' amusement area, as 'The One Bright Spot' in the town. (Lens of Sutton)

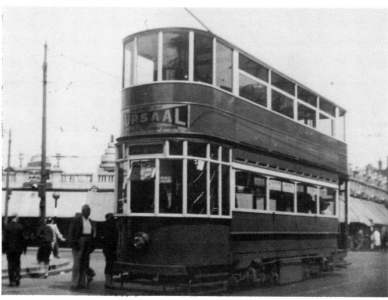

help of many retired employees that a service of sorts was restored on 19th May until the trouble was over. Meantime on 20th April Parliament agreed that the Prittlewell trams could be abandoned in favour of Garrett trolleybuses. Yet for a number of years the trolleybuses could not cope with all the traffic so for a time trams and trolleybuses ran a combined service.

As the 1920s progressed so it was found necessary to improve the comfort of the open-top trams now facing competition from other forms of transport. Once Ministry of Transport objections were overcome to the fitting of top-covers on narrow-gauge tram-cars exposed to the wind, older trams were converted and new cars ordered. But draughts in many top-covered cars caused a constant source of complaint and an experiment to fully vestibule a car proved successful so more were similarly converted. Further trolleybuses were ordered and the routes were extended. Despite this much improvement was made to the central track layout including the Warrior Square loop and additional trams were ordered in 1934. To save costs and to replace older trams, these were bought second-hand with four coming from Middlesborough and three from Accrington.

Economies were still necessary. In January 1934 the livery of the cars was changed to an all-over olive green and early the next year the local service to Thorpe Bay was cut back to the Kursaal leaving the circular services to cope with requirements. The condition of many of the tracks caused anxiety and it was planned that the Boulevard routes should close. In anticipation, a number of well-worn open top cars were scrapped. The last tram ran on the Boulevards on 6th July 1938 with motorbuses taking over the next day. On other routes trolleybuses continued to take precedence.

When the Second World War came in 1939 the trams found a new lease of life as buses were commandeered. Petrol rationing

Car no 53 makes its way along the Thorpe Bay Esplanade seafront in the 1930s not far from Half Way House. During the summer months, there was a service of double-deckers between Thorpe Bay and Leigh along this section of the front. (Lens of Sutton)

Car no 58, built in 1924, seen at Victoria Circus in the 1930s. The tram route carried so many overhead wires at this point that it became known as 'cobweb corner'. Dixons is today the site of W H Smiths. (Lens of Sutton)

caused many bus services to be withdrawn. However, since 1938 no tram service could be terminated or tramcar scrapped without expressed Government approval and certainly with Southend as a front-line town in the defence of Britain and London, no such permission could be easily obtained. It transpired that the winter of 1940 was a severe one and car no 19 (an open top vehicle built in 1904) was taken off passenger services and fitted with snow-ploughs. In the saloon the seats were removed so that salt and sand could be carried. Occasionally services were cancelled during the blitz but no vehicles were lost. The bad state of the track continued to give anxiety and it was blamed for the overturning of car no 57 on 19th December 1941 on the Southchurch route. Fortunately there were no casualties.

Finally, and somewhat inevitably, the Government gave approval on 8th April 1942 for the tram service to end. This stretch of coast was already existing under the tightest possible military security and most non-essential people had left the area. In addition the evacuation of children had long since been completed. To relieve itself from the burden of improving and maintaining the safety of the trams, the corporation had been able to show the dramatic reduction in passengers available to be carried. It was also able to demonstrate that the existing numbers of trolley and motor buses could adequately handle all passenger requirements. With this in mind, the Government gave its approval to the complete closure of the system.

The last tram was driven in pouring rain by Councillor E N Selby, Chairman of the Transport Committee, under the watchful eye of Chief Inspector D J Grimwade who was a conductor when the system began 41 years previously. Speaking to council members and officials later, Councillor Selby told of the many difficulties over the years and thanked those who had overcome them. He announced that during the system's life, some 510 million passengers had been carried and of these not one had been fatally injured. This was surely a wonderful record and a tribute to the tramway men and women.

Today there is little to see of the old system almost 50 years later. A short stretch of tram track used by coal wagons can still be seen on the Corporation Pier and surely further tracks lurk under the present streets. The tram depot has completely gone being today occupied by a branch of Texas Superstore. At the town's central museum a number of tram items have been preserved. Numerous driver and conductor badges together with tickets and tokens have been saved plus also a scholar's pass dated 1918. Best of all perhaps is the length of tram destination blind giving various destinations in the town.

On closure, the *Southend-on-Sea and County Pictorial* commented 'residents will miss for a time the noisy elongated vehicles which were such a familiar feature of our streets but their regret will be tempered by their appreciation of the superior speed and comfort of the trolley and motor buses'. The newspaper concluded, '900 tons of scrap metal have already been contributed to the war effort by removed rails and more will come – soon to join the garden railings in the smelting furnaces'.

Southend-on-Sea Cliff Railway

Whereas the pier tramway at Southend-on-Sea may be well known, the cliff railway is perhaps somewhat less conspicuous. Sited around 500 yards to the west of the Pier it links Western Esplanade with the terrace above saving passengers a sharp climb of almost 60 feet up the cliffside.

The cliff railway at Southend opened in August 1912 rising to a height of 57ft from the esplanade to the terrace above. It was constructed for the Borough by R Waygood & Co Ltd. (Author)

The railway was built in 1912 by R Waygood & Co Ltd for the Borough of Southend and opened in time for the August Bank Holiday crowds. It is unique in that it is a single track operation covering the 130 ft journey on 4 ft 6 in gauge track over a gradient of 1 in 2.3. The firm constructing the railway later became Waygood Otis Ltd and then Otis Elevators Co Ltd which has carried out renovations over the years.

The single car is operated on a counter-balance principle which is today powered by a Waygood Otis Ward Leonard drive system from a 110v DC 3 phase supply. Starting and stopping is by an attendant but the slowing down and final halt works automatically. Safety precautions include an audible alarm which sounds in the pier manager's office in the unlikely event the car stops during its journey.

In April 1990 Otis Elevators supplied a new car to the council which is in use today. The railway (or lift as it is known) is used mainly for elderly or incapacitated people giving them an easier access to the seafront. The past has not been forgotten either since the new car has been designed to the original Edwardian style.

The Electric Tram That Came (to Canvey) and Didn't Stop
Had there not been heavy flooding across Canvey Island during 1904, then a scheme for an electric tramway might well have come about. The man behind the idea was Frederick Hester. In 1899 he bought the farms in the centre and east of the island and set up an estate agency. Hester had plans to turn the area into a residential seaside resort and accordingly marked out plots of land for sale. From the profits he proposed an electric tramway to provide transport from Benfleet Ferry (across the Creek from the railway station) to the Winter Gardens and Leigh Beck.

Every few years high spring tides had brought havoc to the area and it just so happened that when the prospective buyers came to

The numerous tramway artefacts preserved at Southend's Central Museum include this sign board showing the various destinations then available. The collection includes a number of badges and tokens plus a Scholar's Pass of 1918. (Author)

Tram tracks still exist on Corporation Pier off Southchurch Beach Road in September 1990. Southend was one of the few systems that carried coal by tram wagons. From February 1915 coal arriving by sea was taken from the jetty to the municipal power station. (Author)

inspect the various plots then much of the land was found to be under water and could only be viewed from a distance. The thoughtful Hester even provided opera-glasses to those buyers who could not reach their plots at all. Many of the buyers backed out and one, when sued by Hester for the balance of payment, claimed the only way to visit the plot was by balloon!

In *Modern Tramway*, May 1968, J H Price wrote that earlier a temporary horse-powered tramway had run from Benfleet Ferry to Shell Beach. This had been a mono-rail system with the car working on a guide rail principle. The vehicle was kept stable by a horse which walked alongside. It was run partly for prospective plot buyers and partly for summer excursions. The journey was around three miles with much of it through cornfields. According to the late R S Morgan writing in *Essex Countryside*, one of the drivers was a Dutchman dressed in a tall black hat, a tight red jersey and enormous wide pantaloons.

The electric tramway was planned along the strip of land used by the monorail system. Where Hester owned the land, no Parliamentary powers were required but elsewhere a wayleave or easement was probably agreed. During 1904 the Rural District Council agreed that the public road at Leigh Beck could be crossed and in addition the council approved plans for a car shed and generating station. These were proposed at the head of Tewkes Creek where coal could be brought up by barge at high tide.

In February 1904 contracts were placed with an Edinburgh company, Bruce Peebles & Co Ltd, to supply power station equipment, overhead line and six tramcars. Further contracts went to local firms to construct the power house building, the car shed and the track which was to be a single line of 3 ft 6 ins gauge with passing loops. Work on the power station began about March 1904 to supply lighting as well as traction power. A traction engine was acquired and a short length of track was laid near where the depot would be sited. Four cars were needed initially and these were sub-contracted to the Brush Electrical Engineering Co Ltd of Loughborough with motors and controllers believed to be supplied by Ganz & Co of Budapest.

The four cars were single-deck saloons similar to those supplied by Brush for Taunton. Each could seat 24 passengers, 12 each side on longitudinal seats. No record of the livery appears to exist but it is known that one car was inscribed on the rocker panel 'Canvey Island Electric Tramways'. The cars arrived at Benfleet station from Loughborough in mid-1904 to be towed by traction engine to the depot site. It was at this point that a higher-than-usual spring tide took command and the anticipated profits from the proposed land sales did not materialise. When it was known that the plans would fail, Hester stopped work on the tramway and sold up to pay the contractors' claims.

Meantime a tramcar had been delivered but this was hauled back across the ford to Benfleet by horses (the contractor had taken back his traction engine) and returned to Loughborough with the three others. Land in the Winter Gardens area was sold for use for greenhouses and the 3,300 unsold plots went for a mere £2,000 in 1905 to a development company. The company also took over the monorail system although there is no record that it was ever used. It was not until a bus service began operating in 1919 that land began to sell with many receiving old railway vehicles including City & South London tube cars for use as out-buildings.

Early in 1907 two of the tramcars found a use as test cars on the Llandudno & Colwyn Bay Electric Railway but they were later returned to Loughborough. In 1913 there was a possibility the cars might become trailers to York's tramways but this did not materialise. Eventually the trucks were taken for re-use and three of the bodies were broken up, probably during the First World War. One body served a more honourable end as a cricket pavilion.

When the gauge of 3 ft 6 ins was decided upon for Canvey Island, a similar gauge at Southend was borne very much in mind.

Open top cars at the London Road depot. Car no 36's destination board reads 'Cricket Ground' and the front panel advertises Dossett's Gold Medal Pastries. (Lens of Sutton)

The sad sight of cars being demolished in the early 1940s when the system was abandoned. It was claimed that recovery of the tracks provided 900 tons of steel for the war effort. Today the depot site is occupied by Texas Superstore. (Lens of Sutton)

Had the proposals succeeded then the promoters had hoped to build a further line across Benfleet Creek and Hadleigh Marsh to join the Southend trams at Leigh-on-Sea. Instead very little remains at Canvey Island to recall the past. Today a well populated area of over 35,000 people, its only tangible reminder appears to be Station Road at Leigh Beck which exists along the alignment of the tramway that never happened.

Chapter 2

BOAT TRAMS TO
THE LONDON STEAMERS

(Southend Pier Tramway, Walton-on-the-Naze Pier Tramway
and Felixstowe Pier Tramway)

Southend Pier Tramway

A wooden pier was constructed at Southend in 1829–35 and
extended in 1846 to reach the deep water channel in the Thames
Estuary. This was necessary to overcome the vast expanse of mud
that separated the water from the shore at low tide. By 1851 a
narrow-gauge horse tramway had been built along the pier. Initially
this was a cattle truck type car drawn by one horse but as its
popularity increased so further cars were provided. These were
coupled together and pulled by two horses in tandem.

In 1889/90 a new iron pier was built alongside the original
structure and tenders invited to provide an electric tramway. On
Friday, 1st August 1890, the first vehicle, an open cross-bench car
supplied by Cromptons of Chelmsford, had its inaugural run. The
3 ft 6 in gauge third-rail track was then three-quarters of a mile
long and the return journey took ten minutes. Regular running
began on the following day and the public were delighted. Within
three hours around 800 passengers were carried. By the next year a
total distance of 1¼ miles was completed and a set of three cars
was running.

Following the provision of more accommodation on the pier for
steamboats from Tilbury, a prediction was made in 1909 in the
Southend and Westcliff Graphic that the pier would need to be

*Southend Pier, 15th
January 1949, during a
period of single line
working. Note that the
'winter' car has its
sheeting down. (John H
Meredith)*

widened to allow for the laying of double track. The writer also ventured the suggestion that a tunnel might be built under the High Street so that passengers could travel directly to or from the railway station (now the Central Station). This did not of course materialise but by 1913 there were four seven-car trains, the longest ever to run on a British pier tramway.

In the mid-1920s some 25 steamers were calling daily during the summer and the number of passengers using the tramway was almost two million annually. As predicted, the pier was widened by 1929 and the track doubled with colour signalling added. During the Second World War the pier was taken over by the Royal Navy to become known as HMS Leigh. It became the control centre for shipping in the Thames for the duration and, in the event of invasion, there were plans that it should be blown up. Demolition charges were laid ready in place.

The tramway reopened to the public in 1945 and in 1949 four new seven-car trains were obtained. Built by A.C. Cars their design was a cross between the modern Blackpool trams and a London tube train. Traffic reached an all-time high with more than 4,700,000 passengers carried in that year. For a few months the old and the new pier trains worked alongside each other but gradually the old stock was disposed of. Two of the cars, nos 8 and 9, were sold to Brighton corporation where they can be seen today in use on Volks Railway.

The old and the new pass on Southend Pier on 11th June 1949. The press considered the new streamlined trains 'an unnecessary expense' claiming that trippers would not like them. They were proved wrong when up to 55,000 were carried during a single day. (John H Meredith)

As motor transport increased in popularity so steamer traffic along the Thames reduced. Pier traffic declined and from 1970 only two trains were in use. When reconstruction of the pier began in 1974 only one track was used. On 29th July 1976 there was a disastrous fire when the entire pier head facilities were destroyed. Two years later on 2nd October 1978, because of council budget cuts and the poor condition of the track, the pier's famous tramway

Southend Pier's diesel operated tramway, July 1990. The first tramway to travel the pier was electrically operated, having its inaugural run just over a century ago in August 1890. (Author)

closed. In 1980 it seemed that the pier itself was at risk.

Yet all was not lost. Support from the late Sir John Betjeman came for a campaign to save the pier. Sir John said to a local reporter during a visit, 'Closing the Pier would be like cutting off a limb'. A reprieve came in 1983. Funds were made available which, together with fire insurance proceeds, made possible the continuance of the pier and the provision of a new tramway.

Two new trains arrived, each with a locomotive fitted with a 55 hp Deutz diesel engine and five trailer cars. The speed limit was 10 mph and the cars were fitted with ballast to resist the occasional strong winds on the pier. It was a proud day in 1986 when HRH Princess Anne came to Southend to inaugurate the tramway and to formally name the trains after the late Sir William Heygate and, recognising his past interest in the pier, Sir John Betjeman.

It is these trains which regularly travel the pier today with their popularity never ending. Yet no trip to the pier is complete without a visit to the Pier Museum. This was created in 1985 by the Southend Pier Museum Foundation (formerly Friends of Southend Pier Museum). Chairman Peggy Dowie had been a leading campaigner in the fight to save the pier. The Pier Museum opened on 8th July 1989 and it is today governed by a Trust. Here can be found a fascinating collection of Pier memorabilia. These include three carriages preserved from the 1949 tramway and also the chassis and mechanism from the original 1890 tram. Following the discovery in a Benfleet garden of the body of this tram, there is the exciting prospect that this crossbench car can be fully restored in the not too distant future.

Walton-on-the-Naze Pier Tramway

The first tramway to operate along Walton-on-the-Naze's 2,600 ft long pier opened in August 1898. It was a single-line system of 3 ft 6 ins gauge with no passing loops and electrically operated from a centre third rail fed by a 50kW Parker generator. Rolling stock

24

comprised a motor car and two cross-bench 'toast-rack' trailers usually with the three coupled together as one unit. All had been built by the Ashbury Carriage & Iron Co and mounted on Peckham trucks. The motor car's truck was fitted with two 15 hp Crompton motors.

During the 19th century Walton-on-the-Naze (once known as Walton-le-Soken) gained a reputation as a modest Victorian watering place. The resort's first pier, a wooden structure about 300 ft in length, opened in 1830. It was later extended to 800 ft. In May 1867 the Tendring Hundred Railway reached the town causing the population to grow steadily. Walton-on-the-Naze actually preceded nearby Clacton in popularity which did not get any trains until 1882 – at a time when its population was a mere 650.

The 1898 pier opened on the site of the original pier being promoted by the Walton-on-the-Naze Pier and Hotel Ltd. During construction the company became known as the Coast Development Co Ltd, formed as a result of a merger between Belle Steamers Ltd and various other local interests. The tramway lasted until 1935 when it ceased operations. The track was removed and by the next year had been replaced by a rather unusual form of transport.

Visitors to the present-day Metro in Paris may well recall the system that runs on pneumatic-tyred wheels with separate horizontal guide wheels and it was this principle that was adopted at Walton in 1936. A 20-seat cross-bench battery operated vehicle, built by Electricars Ltd, ran in a 6 ft wide trough formed by narrow timber baulking fixed vertically to the deck. Horizontal wheels ran along the sides 'steering' the six-wheeled car along the pier. It could be driven from either end thus the car did not need to be turned at the end of each journey.

On 30th May 1942 the car and much of the pier were destroyed by fire. When rebuilt, a 2 ft gauge contractor's line was laid and in

Southend Pier's tramway track is today single and extends over the full mile and a quarter to the pierhead. For the vigorous it is possible to take a tram out and walk back! (Author)

The motive power on Walton's pier from 1948 came from an 0-4-0 diesel locomotive built by Baguley of Burton-on-Trent, works no 3024/39. It came originally from Wilson's Pleasure Railway at Allhallows, Kent. (John H Meredith)

1948 this was adapted by Walton-on-the-Naze UDC to carry passengers. The system included three bogie toast-rack open coaches with a red and white livery each seating 18. The coaches were hauled by an 0–4–0 diesel-engined locomotive built by Baguley of Burton-on-Trent which came originally from Wilson's Pleasure Railway at Allhallows in Kent.

In recent years it seems the many visitors who have come into Walton either by car or by the single track railway from Colchester have preferred the pier's dodgem cars or perhaps its ghost train. In the early 1980s the rather ageing tramway closed for good and today the only signs of it are the odd pieces of timber baulking scattered about which once guided the electric cars of the 1930s.

Felixstowe Pier Tramway
First ideas for a tramway at Felixstowe came in 1873 when steam traction was authorised. It was proposed that a track should be built from Ipswich railway station to Felixstowe and then on to a pier still to be built. The plans covered 14.67 miles of standard gauge track plus a further 1.4 miles authorised from the pier to Fagborough Head. However the main promoter developed plans for a port at Felixstowe so in 1875 a railway was authorised from Westerfield. When this opened two years later on 1st May 1877 the steam tramway was no longer needed so the idea was dropped. Meantime the pier had been built and, until served by trains, a narrow gauge tramway provided a service between the beach and the pier. This was worked either by horses or a small steam engine hauling two coaches.

In 1903 there were plans at Felixstowe to open an electric tramway on another and more recently built pier. These were proposed by the Coast Development Co Ltd which already oper-ated a pier electric tramway at Walton-on-the-Naze as well as

Walton-on-the-Naze Pier, 28th December 1948. The pier, destroyed by fire in May 1942, was rebuilt after the war and the narrow-gauge contractor's line was adapted for passenger carrying. Note the baulks used by the earlier 'guided rail car' system. (John H Meredith)

owning a fleet of paddle steamers serving the East Coast resorts. Construction of the tramway went ahead and this was duly opened in August 1905.

Like Walton, the gauge was 3 ft 6 ins and the track extended the half-mile length of the new pier. Electricity was supplied from a centre rail which was fed from the council's electricity works. Rolling stock comprised two motor cars and one trailer with all three being of the toast-rack design each seating 36 passengers. The motor cars were fitted with Peckham trucks and they were powered by Thomas Parker motors. Since there was no passing loop, the three cars worked as one unit and the fare was 3d (just over 1p) each way on a service provided only during the summer months.

Later in the year that the tramway opened, the Coast Development Co Ltd was succeeded by the Coast Development Corporation which ten years later went into liquidation. When the company was finally wound up in 1922, both the Pier and the tramway were acquired by East Coast Piers Ltd which continued to provide the usual summer service. In 1926 one of the motor cars was given a new lease of life when it was fitted with a Westinghouse-powered truck taken from an old Ipswich tramcar purchased to provide various parts urgently required.

The tramcar was originally no 34 of the Ipswich fleet which used the same gauge as the pier tramway. It was originally a double-deck open-topped car mounted on a Brush truck and built in 1904. However,not only the truck proved useful since before delivery the top deck had been removed and the saloon section of the car was used as a waiting room at the head of the pier. The car fitted with the 'new' truck continued to serve until 1939 whereas the other vehicles had been scrapped by 1931.

When war broke out in September 1939 services were sus-

After Felixstowe's pier tramway closure in 1939, one of the cars found its way to the amusement park for use as a shelter as seen here on 18th May 1952. (John H Meredith)

pended, never to be re-opened. In 1940 the pier, like many others, was severed as a defence against a possible German invasion and during the years that followed the 'isolated' section became irrevocably damaged by the sea. By 1949 it had reached such a state of collapse that it was demolished. A new shorter pier was built about one third of the length of the original one but it was sadly without trams.

Chapter 3

ASTRIDE THE COLNE

(Colchester Corporation Tramways)

To say that Colchester, once known as *Camulodunum,* has a history could be considered quite an understatement. There was probably a settlement there as early as the 5th century BC and it was in AD 43 that the town was invaded by the Romans who established a major colony. In AD 60 the Britons under Queen Boadicea massacred the Romans and destroyed the temple built by Claudius in AD 50.

It was not until Norman times c1085 that a castle was built on and around the former Roman temple and in 1190 the town's charter was granted by Richard I. Today however the castle keep maintains a more peaceful existence with, as might be expected,

Hythe-bound car no 6 descends St Botolph's Street before turning into Magdalen Street. The system never comprised more than 18 cars during its life and no improvements ever took place. (Lens of Sutton)

St Botolph's Street, Colchester, photographed on a wet September 1990 afternoon. A number of the buildings from the beginning of the century still exist. (Author)

numerous Roman exhibits to be seen. Yet much more up-to-date in the Castle Museum can also be found various tramway artefacts. These include a couple of reversible seats rescued from the Colchester's trams which ceased running well over sixty years ago.

The town's tramway system lasted just 25 years with a public service commencing on 28th July 1904. The official opening was held in pouring rain yet despite this a large crowd collected to watch the Mayoress drive the first car (no 13) from the Town Hall to Lexden, then to North Station and finally back to the Town Hall. The car was decorated with flags and bunting and it carried many invited guests and led a procession of four cars.

Had an earlier company survived then Colchester might well have had a steam tramway. In 1883 Parliament approved a Provisional Order for such a system and track laying proceeded between North Station and the High Street but by the time it reached Middleborough the company had run into financial difficulties and the plans were dropped. The track was removed and forfeited to Colchester Corporation along with all other materials.

In 1898 the British Electric Traction Company (BET) applied for a Light Railway Order to allow the introduction of of electric trams on five short routes emanating from the town centre. The application was rejected by the Light Railway Commissioners on the grounds that the routes were all within the borough. The Commissioners stated that the system should be promoted as an urban tramway to be authorised under the Tramways Act of 1870. Further ideas came forward including an interesting idea in 1901. The Board of Trade approved a proposal from Colchester Town Council to run 'cars or omnibuses' by overhead electric wires – but without the laying of track. Thus Colchester could have become the first town in Britain to operate trolleybuses! Subsequently

JI/90

Colchester car no 3 about to descend North Hill bound for North Station. Because of the 1 in 12 gradient, all Colchester's trams were fitted with track brakes. (Lens of Sutton)

Parliament agreed an Act of 1901 authorising Colchester Corporation to build and work a system using 3 ft 6 in gauge electric trams within the borough.

A number of town councillors were unsure about the decision and decided to wait and see how motor buses developed. The buses proved unreliable although it was not until February 1903 that a vote of 18 to 9 agreed that an electric tramway should be built at an estimated cost of around £63,000. Also in 1901 there had been a proposal from a company to build a light railway from Southend to Colchester. It was expected the promoters would seek a link with the Colchester system but since the light railway proposed a gauge of 4 ft 8½ in and the town's gauge was 3 ft 6 in, there would have been difficulties.

The fleet initially comprised 16 cars supplied at a cost of £575 each. They were built by the Electric Railway & Tramway Carriage Works Ltd and mounted on Brill trucks. The cars were four-wheeled and open-topped with three main windows on each side. Each seated 22 passengers in the saloon where the seats were longitudinal and a further 24 'on top'. The livery was dark brown and cream and the current collection was by overhead trolley which was set to one side of the car. The staircases were reversed and destination boards were fitted high above the front deck rails.

Within a month of opening there were complaints from the local clergy and ministers who wanted trams suspended during church services on Sundays. This was a common complaint in many towns including a number of clergymen who were concerned that the noise of the passing trams drowned the words of their sermons. Colchester Corporation held a lively debate on the issue but decided by a small majority that nothing should be done.

Tram routes covered services from North Station to Lexden,

East Gates and Hythe. In 1905 Parliament agreed an extension of single track from St Botolph's to the recreation ground. Again trams covered this route from the North Station and to cover the extra service, two further cars (nos 17 and 18) were obtained but not built by the United Electric Car Co Ltd. Unlike the earlier cars they had direct staircases. The fleet now comprised a total of 18 cars and no further cars were bought during the system's life.

At the top of Queen Street at the junction with High Street single track was necessary along the curve in the road. To avoid cars meeting, a signalling system was installed although it was necessary for the driver to switch on the signal when entering the section and switch it off again when leaving. Fares were in 1d (less than ½p) sections with a typical cost of 1d to travel from North Station to the top of North Hill.

The trams led a fairly uneventful existence although there was a problem in 1908 when a car caught the handle of a blind man's barrel organ turning it over. In consequence the organist sued the Corporation for £14 15s (£14.75) while the latter claimed obstruction. It was finally settled out of court without the Corporation admitting liability. Another occasion proved a happier one when car no 10 was highly decorated to carry a wedding party. However, when the 1914–1918 war came the tramway, like many others, suffered problems. The condition of the track grew steadily worse and no work was carried out on any of the cars.

Even after the war no modernisation took place and in 1927 the Corporation decided to terminate the system. A Bill was presented to Parliament which authorised the abandonment of the trams and agreed the operation of trolleybuses on the tramway routes and the use of motor buses elsewhere within the borough. No trolleybuses were ever run in Colchester but a number of offers to operate bus services were received from private companies. However, the Corporation decided to go ahead with a scheme of its own to replace the trams with motor buses. Even so a number of private operators ran buses within the borough before the passing of the Act and the

The saloon body of a Colchester tram currently in use as a garden shed at a private residence in the village of Great Horkesley. It is believed to be either car no 6 or car no 9. (Author)

fares were generally 50% higher than on the trams.

Over the next two years the sections of tramway gradually gave way to Corporation buses. The last tram ran to Lexden on 30th September 1928 and in the summer of 1929 the section between North Station and the top of North Hill was abandoned because of the poor condition of the track. In the same year the Corporation agreed that the private bus operators could continue but fares would be charged at the same rate as the Corporation buses for all journeys within the borough. In return the private operators paid the Corporation 25% of their receipts.

The last tram in Colchester ran on 8th December 1929 by which time all routes were covered by buses. It was not long before most of the rails were lifted although some were covered over as the roads were reinstated. At the same time the tram depot in Magdalen Street was converted for use by buses. The majority of the car bodies were sold to a local builder who used them as site huts. Some survived to be used as garden sheds and today one of these can still be found in the garden of a private residence at the village of Great Horkesley just off the A134 from Colchester to Sudbury.

Currently in use as a garden shed, only the saloon body exists. According to R C Anderson in his book *The Tramways of East Anglia*, it could be the body of either car 6 or car 9 both of which were known to have survived until 1963 at least in local villages. Unfortunately examination of the body gives no indication of the number although most of the windows and the end doors are intact. Unhappily some of the woodwork is in poor condition.

At the Magdalen Street depot, sections of tram track can still be seen. The shed carried six roads and when the inspection pits were recently extended for use by buses, Mr Sampson, the depot's director, was besieged by enthusiasts who sought sections of the redundant track. The workshop obliged by cutting pieces into 6 inch to 9 inch sections for the 'buffs'!

Not long ago during a clearout at the depot offices, specifications were found among the dust and dirt dating back to before the start of the trams in 1904. In addition there were copies of engineers' reports to the Corporation dated 1927/8 prepared during the proposed change from trams to either trolleybuses or motor buses. The costing was detailed down to the last ½d (about a fifth of 1p).

The workshops at the depot once served as stables for horses used at the nearby St Botolph's railway station which had been brought into use on 1st March 1866 by the Tendering Hundred Railway. In the late 1970s the gulleys under the depot's inspection pits were examined and it was found to the surprise of all concerned that a tunnel (now blocked for obvious security reasons) linked the pits with the railway station a hundred yards or so away.

Chapter 4

NARROW TRAMS FOR NARROW STREETS

(Ipswich Corporation Tramways)

A visit to the old Priory Heath Bus depot in Ipswich's Cobham Road in September 1990 truly seemed a visit into the past. Pride of place for a tram enthusiast was the saloon body of double deck open top tramcar no 33 on a loader near the entrance. Built by Brush of Loughborough in 1904, it had survived the years well despite the fact a good part of its life was spent as a storeshed at Claydon, a village just north of the town. Car no 33's three main windows each side were intact and the words 'Ipswich Corporation Tramways' could just be determined on the side. There was also evidence of the gold lining on some of the platform panels. A notice inside the saloon had read 'Do not tender gold coins'.

The Priory Heath depot began life in 1936 housing trolleybuses but when it closed in 1987 it was accommodating motor buses. For a time it was used as a paint shop and work shop. Although now occupied by the Ipswich Transport Museum, it is not normally open to the public due to the terms of the licence but open days are held and there are regular preservation working sessions to which serious volunteers are invited.

Another delight to be found is the oldest known trolleybus fully restored to its original livery. I.C.T trolleybus no 2, DX 3988, was built in 1923, the body by Shorts of Rochester and the chassis by

Horse tram tracks in evidence at the Quadling Street depot when visited in September 1990. If planning permission is granted, the premises, owned by John Woods (Transport) Ltd, will be converted to a car park. (Author)

Railless Ltd. It has not quite been restored as originally for it previously had an open backed end for smokers. Further trolleybuses appear among the numerous exhibits with another, a Ransomes B3OD, dating back to 1926. It is interesting to recall that the people of Ipswich called their trolleybuses 'trams' at a time when elsewhere they were referred to as 'trolleys'. With Ipswich an early operator of electric buses, they were regarded as 'trackless trams'.

Another aspect of the past was found at the premises of John Woods (Transport) Ltd in Quadling Street not far from the railway station. When visited in September 1990 tracks leading into the yard could be seen – tracks that were once used by horse trams – but the wooden depot which housed the trams was no longer there. Because it had become unsafe, it had been removed to the Cobham Road depot piece by piece by Manpower Services and stored until time and effort can be found to restore it. Each piece of wood had been carefully labelled and the original site extensively photographed so that hopefully one day the shed could be rebuilt. Yet at Quadling Street other buildings had survived. The stables,

The same scene in September 1990. The Wolsey Pharmacy has become an international firm of auctioneers and valuers and the trams (and the trolleybuses) have long since gone. (Author)

offices, tack room and the manager's house were still there although one wondered for how much longer. Planning permission was being sought for demolition and the use of the site as a car park – a sad day indeed for historians should such a valuable area be given up.

Horse trams came to Ipswich to meet the needs of a rapidly growing population. A gauge of 3 ft 6 ins was chosen and the first line was constructed in the Spring of 1880 from Cornhill to the railway station. The opening was delayed since after completion the contractor had been declared bankrupt. The first tramcar, a single-deck car built by Starbuck of Birkenhead, arrived in August 1880 and the Mayor and Town Clerk were passengers on a trial run. During its journey it came off the rails – much to the amusement of the local cabbies who viewed the trams as potential rivals.

The grand opening came on Wednesday, 13th October 1880. The fare was 2d (just under 1p) which passengers dropped into a locked tin box and the journey was comparatively comfortable since red velvet cushions were provided. At first there were two single-deck four-wheeled cars which had to be stored at either end of the line when not in use. Land for a yard was not obtained until several days later, on 18th October 1880 and the Quadling Street depot was not constructed until 1883. The livery was maroon and cream with the name 'Ipswich Tramway Company' on the rocker panels.

In March 1881 horse trams were reaching Brooks Hall Road via Portman Road and Norwich Road. Their popularity was undoubted since over 1000 passengers were carried on the Easter Monday Bank Holiday of that year. To meet increased demand, two further cars were ordered, one a four-wheeled double-deck car, open-topped with back-to-back (knifeboard) seating along the centre. The following year a route between Barrack Corner and Cornhill was opened which meant that cars to Brooks Hall Road could run via the Cornhill. When trams reached Derby Road station in the summer of 1883 the service was complete. To cover this route two double-deck cars were each hauled by two horses but with a third horse attached to pull the car up the hill at St John's Road. By the mid-1880s the tramway company owned eight cars and eighteen horses to cover the four miles of track.

In 1893 the horse trams were withdrawn from service for two weeks because the company refused to accept the corporation's terms for repairing the roads. The wood paving between the rails had deteriorated badly, particularly in Westgate Street and St Matthew's Street. Since tramway companies under an Act of 1870 were held responsible for the condition of the roadway between the rails and up to 18 ins each side of the track, the corporation had served notice for the work to be done. The repair bill came to £832 and the corporation eventually agreed to carry out the work against payment by the company of £100 per year after which services were resumed. During the trams' absence, local cab proprietors were of course quick to take advantage of the situation. Despite the company's problems, a further double-deck car was purchased in 1896 for £158 and three single-deck cars were converted to double-deckers.

On 20th June 1898 Ipswich saw bright red horse-drawn buses on its streets offering cheap fares and frequent journeys. They were known locally as the 'Penny Omnibuses' and they were able to cover new routes thus competing strongly with the trams. In addition the buses ran on Sundays which the trams had never done. The tramway company retaliated by reducing its fares but its finances remained very strained. Attempts by the company to sell its concern to another company proved unsuccessful and in 1901 the corporation served a compulsory purchase order allowed under the 1870 Tramways Act. The price was eventually settled by arbitration at £17,552. The corporation took over the responsibility of running the horse trams from 1st November 1901. They lasted only until 6th June 1903 when, hardly a financial success, they ceased running to make way for electric trams in the town.

Cornhill and Tavern Street, c1910. Electric trams lasted in Ipswich until July 1926 when they were replaced by trolleybuses. (Lens of Sutton)

37

The authority to provide this 'new form of traction' came with the passing of the Ipswich Corporation Tramways Act 1900. As soon as the horse trams stopped, the old rails were lifted which meant that no trams ran for several months. This provided a haven for the horse bus operators although the widespread road works gave many problems. Meantime the horse trams were sold off to become shepherd's huts and chicken sheds and the like.

A major consideration in deciding to maintain the gauge of 3 ft 6 ins was the town's narrow streets. In addition there were many curves, particularly one at Major's Corner with a radius of 40 ft, although gradients were not severe. The permanent-way construction was carried out by Dick, Kerr & Co Ltd providing in all 10.82 route miles at a cost of £41,220. To commence the service 26 double-deck open-top Brush cars were acquired each powered by two 25 hp Westinghouse motors. Current collection was from overhead wires and the cars were painted dark green and cream, outlined in gold and black, with the fleet number on each dash. In the centre of the waist panel was the corporation crest and on the rocker panel was written 'Ipswich Corporation Tramways'. A feature of the cars was that they had an overall width of 5 ft 9 ins making them at the time the narrowest used in this country.

The weather was poor for the official opening on 21st November 1903 when Mrs Fred Bennett, the Mayoress, opened the main doorway at the tramway offices with a silver key to declare the Ipswich Corporation Tramways open. A civic lunch was held in the specially decorated repair shop after which the guests were given a special tour to Whitton. Many local residents turned out to watch these 'five cars aglow with electric lights'. Unfortunately a number of minor mishaps occurred around the time the service began. On a trial run at night on 10th November 1903 car no 22 had left the

rails because of a faulty point setting. On the day public services began, Monday, 23rd November, car no 20 left the rails at the top of Princes Street and it took two further cars to get it right again. The following day there was a power failure but fortunately after this such misfortunes became rare.

The trams were immediately popular and crowds gathered at the Cornhill to watch them pass. On the first day the only route open was from Whitton to Bourne Bridge (via Cornhill and Ipswich station) together with a spur off Wherstead Road along Bath Street to reach the river steamers. Further routes to Lattice Barn, Derby Road station and along Bramford Road followed on 21st December on which date the 'Penny Omnibuses' were discontinued. In May 1904 the system was completed when trams reached the Royal Oak via Bishops Hill and Felixstowe Road. To meet the extra demand ten further open-topped Brush cars were ordered making 36 in all.

Fares ranged between 1d and 3d (less than ½p to just over 1p) with tickets being the Bell punch type cancelled at the printed stages by hand-operated punches. Ipswich Corporation also sold books of pre-paid tickets which were exchanged during travel for an ordinary ticket of the same value. Tram stops, familiar to many towns, were clearly marked as 'Fare Stage', 'Cars stop if required' or 'All Cars Stop'. In August 1905 half-fares were introduced before 8 am.

The First World War, as with all systems, meant staff shortages and spare parts virtually unobtainable. With paint soon in short supply, a number of cars were painted grey overall. Ten were affected but only one (no 36) returned to its original livery at a later date. The remaining cars painted grey were used on special workmen's services. In 1917 the short branch along Bath Street

Trams at the Ipswich Great Eastern Railway station not long after the system opened. From the picture it looks as though the trolley arm (just out of the picture) has come off the overhead wire. (Colin Withey collection)

was closed and the rails removed since new track could not be purchased. The poles remained to distribute electricity to the local houses.

After the war the track was in a badly worn state, partly due to the heavy industrial traffic required to pass through the town's narrow streets during wartime. Much of the damage had been caused by horse-drawn vehicles with metal tyres. Due to the heavy costs for renewal there was soon a call to 'scrap the trams'. At the same time Thomas Tilling motor buses had started services although their licence stipulated a minimum fare within the Borough to protect the trams.

Certain tracks were relaid in 1921 when rails were again available but ideas to end the trams persisted. As a result of this, Ipswich Corporation hired three Railless/English Electric trolleybuses which commenced services between the Cornhill and Ipswich station on 2nd September 1923. Consequently the trams along the route ceased operation but since overhead wires already existed, only an additional negative wire was needed. The trolleybuses were two-motor single-deck vehicles each with 30 seats which included eight in an open-ended compartment at the rear for smokers. The trolleybuses worked as pay-as-you-enter vehicles and were one-man-operated.

The trolleybuses proved successful so the three vehicles were purchased. The track in Princes Street was removed and the road resurfaced. Ipswich Corporation had become one of the first in the country to convert a route from tram to trolleybus operation. When a fourth single-deck trolleybus was acquired in 1924 it was made by Ransomes, Sims & Jefferies, an Ipswich company. The Eastern Counties Road Car Co Ltd (previously Thomas Tilling) were not unexpectedly concerned at the potential competition and offered to provide a fleet of motor buses to the corporation. In addition the company stated its willingness to pay the corporation £6,000 a year for 20 years in return for the four trolleybuses and it also sought protection against competition from the trams. The council were

The former tram depot at Constantine Road is today used by Ipswich Buses. The old tram tracks were taken out as recently as 1987 and filled over. (Author)

Ipswich trolleybus DX8871 built by Ransomes, Sims & Jefferies in 1930 can be seen at the East Anglia Transport Museum at Carlton Colville. (Author)

Also at the Priory Heath depot can be found the oldest known trolleybus DX3988 built in 1923. It has been fully restored to its original livery. (Author)

not happy about the offer so a referendum was held. The rate-payers decided by 3,780 votes to 2,156 votes to keep the trolleybuses so, during 1925, another single-deck experimental vehicle was purchased.

Ipswich Corporation applied for Royal Assent to replace its trams by trolleybuses and this was received on 7th August 1925. After a final experimental vehicle, a Ransomes dual-entrance single-decker was received the corporation was able to consider what makes to purchase. Gradually the tramway routes were taken over and when the last car ran on 26th July 1926 the conversion was complete. The corporation were operating with 15 Ransomes single-deck dual-entrance trolleybuses and 15 similar Garrett vehicles. The electric trams at Ipswich had served for less than 23 years.

In the early 1930s the experimental vehicles were withdrawn and the first double-deck trolleybuses were introduced. In 1936

the depot at Priory Heath opened serving trolleybuses which were to survive on many of the town's streets until August 1963. When vehicle no 114 made a last journey to the depot it carried the letters RIP painted on its side.

Apart from the 1923 trolleybus DX3988 surviving at the old Priory Heath depot, another can be found at the East Anglia Transport Museum at Carlton Colville. This is single-deck trolleybus no 44 DX8871 built by Ransomes dating from 1930. It came to Carlton Colville in 1974 from the Clapham transport museum with its destination board still serving as a reminder of the past. It reads LATTICE BARN 3A.

Chapter 5

TRAMS ACROSS A SWING BRIDGE

(Lowestoft Corporation Tramways)

There was great excitement among tram enthusiasts at the end of 1988 when a Lowestoft bungalow was put up for sale. Built into the back of the bungalow was discovered the body of a 1904 vintage tram in an excellent state of preservation for its age. The single-deck car, one of only four built, was originally in service between 1904 and 1931 after which it was sold off to become a garden chalet. During that time it acquired a professionally-built pitched roof and it was well painted to protect it from all weathers.

The bungalow's new owner happily agreed to part with the tram body so in January 1990 it was carefully winched onto a low-loader after which it was slowly transported to a new resting place at the East Anglia Transport Museum at Carlton Colville. The removal had been no easy task. All means had been considered including a possible lift by helicopter but this would have proved very costly. Finally the hauliers, V C Cooke & Sons Ltd of Beccles, proved very helpful by lifting the body and carrying it to the museum.

The single-deck tram body is not the only relic from Lowestoft's tramways. Another tram at Carlton Colville is car no 14 which was rescued for preservation in 1961. This is a double-deck open-topped car built by Milnes in 1904 for the town's 3 ft 6 ins gauge tramway. It spent many years as a summer house before being

Car no 8 in Lowestoft's London Road not long after the tramway system began in 1903. The town's trams lasted almost 28 years. (Lens of Sutton)

restored to the present fine condition of today. The car's present truck is standard gauge to allow operation on the museum's track.

Trams were first considered in Lowestoft when the Yarmouth & Gorleston Tramways Company obtained powers to build and work a horse-tramway system within the borough but the scheme never materialised. Just before the turn of the century in 1898 the East Anglian Light Railway Company (EALR), a subsidiary of Drake & Gorham Electric Power & Traction Co Ltd, proposed a chain of electric tramways to run from Caister to Great Yarmouth and Lowestoft and then through Kessingland to Southwold. Lowestoft council supported the idea but only agreeing a route from Gorleston via Lowestoft to Kessingland. There was also a stipulation that gave the council powers to purchase that part of the tramway within its Borough at intervals of 7, 14, 21 or 28 years plus the receipt of 10% of the profits.

In May 1899 the Great Eastern Railway and Great Northern Railway Joint Committee voiced strong criticism of the project at a public enquiry, pointing out that it already had powers to construct a railway over the Yarmouth to Lowestoft part of the route. In consequence the proposal to build a tramway north of Lowestoft's swing bridge was turned down but the Light Railway Commissioners recommended that the EALR should construct a tramway from south of the swing bridge to Kessingland but this proposal was rejected. After lengthy negotiations between the EALR and Lowestoft council, it was decided that the council should itself obtain powers to construct and work an electric tramway from the northern boundary to the southern boundary of the borough. Although the council took over the EALR's powers to extend to Kessingland, the section southwards from Pakefield was never built.

Construction work began in 1903 after a lengthy delay in delivery of the rails. They had been loaded into a sailing barge at Antwerp and then had to be towed across the North Sea by a German tug. Once received the work went ahead with the first rail

London Road c1906 before the age of the motor car. The town's fleet comprised at most 15 double-deck and four single-deck cars. (Lens of Sutton)

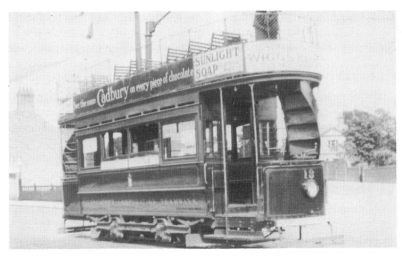

laid at a special ceremony on 11th March 1903. The Mayoress received a souvenir for the occasion in the shape of a paper weight with a silver model of the tramway track on a granite bed and housed in a case. It was suitably inscribed giving the date and the event. In a speech given later, the Mayor referred to the delay in receiving the rails and pointed out that to have the trams ready for the summer season, work was necessary by day and night. He hoped the High Street residents would not be upset if they lost too much sleep.

Much of the 3 ft 6 ins gauge track was single with passing places and current collection was by the conventional overhead wire system. The total route length came to just over four miles running from Yarmouth Road to the north, via the High Street and London Road to cross the swing bridge. To the south the trams travelled along London Road South to reach the terminus at a junction with Florence Road at Pakefield. Trams reached a depot built in Rotterdam Road by a branch along Denmark Street from the main route. A service along this short section existed for a time but this was withdrawn after three weeks through lack of demand.

Construction work to allow the crossing by trams of the 40 ft swing bridge, erected by the Great Eastern Railway in 1897, proved complicated. When the bridge opened, using its hydraulic power, it first tilted then swung upon a pivot. For this reason the tramway overhead line equipment had to be built so that it swung with the bridge as one unit. As a precaution a system was incorporated so that when the bridge opened, the overhead line on the bridge and for a suitable distance each side automatically cut out. Catch points were also installed and barriers were placed across the approach. With such devices it was apparent that no tram could approach the bridge when it was open for shipping.

Following the supply of eleven four-wheel open-top double-deck cars and 4 bogie single-deck cars, all from Milnes, trial tests began over the route. These happened at night giving, it was claimed, further disturbed nights for residents living nearby.

However, their troubles were short-lived for inspection of the system by the Board of Trade soon followed and the grand opening day was fixed for Wednesday, 22nd July 1903. Once again the Mayor and Mayoress were present for the occasion with many invitations sent out to make up the official party. The first tram was bedecked with flags and evergreens, with flowers festooned around the windows. When it left the depot shortly after noon, many people lined the decorated route. It was the first of a procession of four cars which travelled to the Yarmouth Road terminus, then south to Pakefield and finally back to the Grand Hotel where the party celebrated with an official lunch.

The system was then opened to the public with a seven minute service in operation. Needless to say it was well patronised with over 165,000 passengers carried in the first two weeks. In 1904 four more double-deck cars were purchased, again from Milnes, giving the fleet its maximum of 19 cars in all, plus a Brush sweeper/sprinkler. Their livery was described as Munich lake and cream but the works car was painted grey. Four of the cars were single-deckers capable of seating 50 passengers and equipped with an open smoking compartment at each end. They were not regularly used being known as 'winter cars' and they also had an unfortunate tendency to derail on sharp bends.

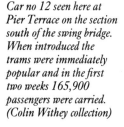

Car no 12 seen here at Pier Terrace on the section south of the swing bridge. When introduced the trams were immediately popular and in the first two weeks 165,900 passengers were carried. (Colin Withey collection)

Despite the trams' initial popularity, all did not go well in the years that followed largely because of troubles experienced with road foundations. A lot of money had to be spent on repair work. In 1910 through lack of passengers it was necessary to terminate the northern end at North Parade instead of along Yarmouth Road. In addition the through 1d (less than ½p) fare was increased to 2d with 1d stages introduced. In 1912 the condition of the track had

deteriorated to the extent that a thorough renovation was necessary. This cost the council £10,000 which had to be borrowed over a fifteen year period. By 1913 the tramway had built up a deficit of £26,000 and fares were raised once again.

The First World War saw the usual shortage of male employees so women drivers, conductors and inspectors were introduced. As with other systems, materials for maintenance were also in short supply. Yet around that time there were two amusing happenings regarding animals. In his book, *The Tramways of East Anglia*, R C Anderson wrote that just before the First World War a car approached a stop and waiting to board was an Italian circus master with a dancing bear. The conductor was not happy about having a bear in his car but, after consultation with the driver, it was agreed the Italian and his bear could travel on the top deck with the animal considered in the same category as a dog. Immediately all the other passengers fled downstairs. Left alone, and much to the surprise of passengers waiting along the route, the circus master played a tune on his accordion and encouraged the bear to jump about. No trouble was caused and no action was taken against the driver and conductor concerned but an instruction was issued subsequently stating that in future bears were not allowed to travel on cars.

The second incident occurred a short time after the war. A circus promoter asked if a baby elephant could be carried by tram from Pakefield to the town centre. The tramway manager agreed to this so the car floor was strengthened and the elephant was carried for the normal adult fare of 2d!

In 1920 poles and span wires were installed along Rotterdam Road and Normanston Drive in anticipation of trolleybus operation but no overhead wires were ever erected. The corporation had obtained powers to operate trolleybuses and motor buses earlier that year with plans that trolleybuses should reach new areas including Oulton. In the end only a corporation bus service was introduced – and then not until 1927 when a sea-front service began. The few poles and span wires erected for the trolleybuses

A view of the upper deck of Lowestoft 14 at Carlton Colville. Travelling 'on top' was only for the sturdy during wintry weather! (Author)

Lowestoft car no 14 resides today at the East Anglia Transport Museum at Carlton Colville. Built by Milnes in 1904, it spent many years as a summer house after its 'retirement' before being restored to its present fine condition. (Author)

were used to support overhead lighting. The motor buses operated what became known as a 'sea wall' service with open saloons available throughout the summer at half-hourly intervals. A poster of the day read: 'Lowestoft Corporation Transport. Motor Omnibus Service will run daily By the Silvery Sea'.

In 1928 the bus service extended to cover further areas and in 1929 a half-hourly bus service was introduced along the tramway route and beyond to reach the northern borough boundary. It was becoming apparent that the trams were outliving their usefulness and in 1930 it came as no surprise when the corporation decided to abandon the system in favour of motor buses rather than re-equip and extend the line. On 10th April 1931 removal of the track on the northern section began while trams continued for a time to cover the section to Pakefield.

The last tram in Lowestoft ran on 8th May 1931, driven by the oldest driver who had served the tramway since it began in 1903. As with the system's inauguration, large crowds turned out but this time the final car carried a huge wreath of lilies heavily bordered and crossed with black. Today, apart from the two cars at the East Anglia Transport Museum, the main reminder of the earlier days is the tram depot which survives in Rotterdam Road. Currently in industrial use, the building was constructed in red brick with stone facings. It could accommodate 16 cars on four roads each with a full length inspection pit. A fifth track at right angles near the entrance was added later. A track was also built along Rotterdam Road to reach near the junction with Norwich Road but this was removed by 1926.

Lowestoft could be proud of its tramway service. It lasted almost 28 years and during that time carried some 80 million passengers with a car mileage of around 8 million miles!

Chapter 6

TRAMS DIVIDED BY A BRIDGE

(Great Yarmouth Corporation Tramways)

Great Yarmouth, renowned for many years as a great herring port and today a popular holiday centre, is a long town stretched out over miles of the Norfolk coast. Yet unlike Lowestoft, the tramway system of Great Yarmouth was split into two since the bridge across the river Yare was not suitable for trams. The bridge remained a narrow wooden structure until 1930 with the centre span being raised and lowered by hand winches. However the towns did share the possibility in 1898 of a light railway system from Caister through Yarmouth and Lowestoft to Southwold but this did not materialise.

Before the arrival of the trams, the only way to get about in Great Yarmouth, apart from walking, was by a vehicle known as Limmer's omnibus which regularly plied between Feather's Plain and the Buck Inn. When the first tramway came in April 1875 it was a horse-operated system which offered a service from South-town railway station (Haven Bridge) to the Feather's Plain at Gorleston. Later a summer service was extended to Brush Quay. The gauge was 4 ft 8½ ins and the rails were laid on wooden sleepers. Yet there was opposition to the trams especially from the cab drivers. One night during the construction of the track a strong party of roughs overcame the watchman and threw a number of rails into the river from the Bollard Quay.

The horse trams ran at 15 minute intervals but the going was slow. It was reported that the journey was as 'pleasant and easy as

Car no 6 at Market Place turning towards Theatre Plain, c1910. The track through the market was relaid and doubled in 1913. (Lens of Sutton)

one could desire'. First class passengers were given the innermost seats just behind the driver with the additional amenity of having 'extra straw to keep the feet warm in wintry weather'. Despite such 'comfort' it could take up to 2½ hours to complete a single journey. There had earlier been plans to reach as far south as Halesworth – one shudders to think how long such a ride might have taken.

In 1878 the company was acquired by the Yarmouth & Gorleston Tramways Co which in 1882 relaid the track in concrete and to a gauge of 3 ft 6 ins. By this time the fleet consisted of ten horse-drawn double-deck cars each capable of seating 46 people. In addition the company operated a number of double-deck horse buses. Despite several extensions being added, the route length never exceeded 2¾ miles. A depot was built at Gorleston plus stables which could accommodate the stud of 68 horses.

In the years that followed the concern suffered financially with the shareholders losing some £17,500. In 1896 pressure was growing for a municipal tramway and in 1898 the corporation successfully applied for Parliamentary powers to construct its own electric tramway. Competition came in 1900 from the British Electric Traction Company (BET) which acquired the horse tram company at less than 75% of its par value but its various attempts to apply for powers to electrify the system were vetoed by the corporation which was going ahead anyway with its own system.

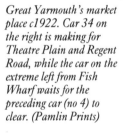

Great Yarmouth's market place c1922. Car 34 on the right is making for Theatre Plain and Regent Road, while the car on the extreme left from Fish Wharf waits for the preceding car (no 4) to clear. (Pamlin Prints)

Meantime, because of general demand, steel prices had risen and no further action was taken until the autumn of 1901 when the corporation invited quotations for the supply of rails. The successful company came from Belgium with its offer far lower than any British firm.

Work began on 16th October 1901 on a complex of lines from the Caister Road depot. This included a route to Marine Parade

Car 13 passes along Marine Parade bound for Wellington Pier. As motor buses were introduced during the 1920s so tram routes were closed. The last tram between Vauxhall Station and Wellington Pier ran on 6th October 1929. (Lens of Sutton)

reaching Wellington pier and a branch to Vauxhall railway station returning via the quays and Regent Street. The gauge was 3 ft 6 ins and the overhead line system was used. A Board of Trade inspection was carried out on 19th June 1902 when the tramway was passed as suitable for public service. That afternoon three cars suitably decorated toured the crowded route. One of the cars must have been quite a spectacle for it carried on its top deck the band of the Prince of Wales' Own Norfolk Artillery. The following day, Friday, 20th June 1902, a full public service was available.

The first batch of 14 cars arrived for the opening from Brush of Loughborough. These were four-window open-top four-wheeled vehicles each seating 56 passengers and equipped with two 25 hp motors. The lower deck had longitudinal seats while 'on top' they were wooden reversible garden-type seats. The livery was maroon and cream and the corporation's coat of arms was displayed on the centre of the (maroon) upper side panel with the words 'Gt. Yarmouth Corporation Tramways' on the (cream) rocker panel.

Short extensions to the route were added in 1904/5. There were also plans to build a subway under the river Yare or alternatively rebuild the river bridge but nothing was done and not at any time did trams cross the river. In September 1905 a decision was taken to widen the bridge but again nothing came of it. Trams commenced services from Haven Bridge to Gorleston on 4th July 1905 and the two parts of the town's tramway system remained divided throughout.

To operate the Gorleston section 10 new open-top cars were supplied, again from Brush, and a further two allocated to north of the bridge. The opening of the Gorleston section meant of course the end of the horse trams so an auction was held at Southtown's Yareside Stables. The horses were sold at prices reaching 35 guineas (£36.75) and a number of trams were sold off to private residents at prices ranging between 8 and 10½ guineas (between £8.40 and £11). Some of the better known horses had acquired names such as 'Polly', 'Smasher', 'Bess' or even 'Lopsy Popsy'.

An extension opened in the northern section reached Fish Wharf on 8th August 1905 and during 1906 five further cars were purchased from Brush. When a final major extension to cross the borough boundary to Caister opened on 16th May 1907 the systems were virtually complete with almost 10 route miles of track. To meet the extra demand, now Caister's developing sea front and cemetery were reached, four further Brush cars were acquired making a total of 35 in all. Trams on the Southtown to Gorleston route provided a 15 minute service in the winter, improved to every 7½ minutes in the summer months carrying many passengers on to Gorleston Beach. On the northern section trams ran between Wellington Pier and Caister every 15 minutes. Colour signals protected four sections of single track and 'Next Car' clocks were installed at three locations. In addition, ten 'waiting shelters' were erected along the route.

The First World War gave the problems experienced by most tramway undertakings with shortages of parts and staff. No new cars were purchased and most of the cash available went on repairs and track replacements. In 1920 the Tramway Committee decided to consider motor buses with the result that three second-hand open-top double-deck vehicles were purchased from the London General Omnibus Co Ltd for £1,725. A bus service began on 20th October 1920 to support the existing tram service on routes between Vauxhall station and Wellington Pier. The buses carried advertisements, one of these ironically reading 'Travel by Tram'.

The introduction of buses led to the abandonment of tram services from Newtown to Fish Wharf on 14th May 1924. On that day trams also stopped running along St Peter's Road as well as along Fullers Hill between Vauxhall station and Church Plain. Track renewal also became necessary elsewhere causing heavy financial commitments on the undertaking. As further buses were introduced during the late 1920s, so the tram service from Vauxhall station to Wellington Pier terminated on 6th October 1929.

When closure of the tram service from Southtown to Gorleston

Great Yarmouth's Town Hall and Quay not long after electric trams began in June 1902. The track on the righthand side of the road served Great Eastern Railway trains on a branch to Fish Wharf. (Lens of Sutton)

was announced in May 1930 there were immediate questions. 'What will happen to the crowds who packed the trams when there will only be limited accommodation on the buses?' some asked. The Tramway Committee said they would do their best until further buses arrived. 'But what are the folk with infants going to do?' asked the mothers who had often been able to leave their prams on the driver's platform. A wit unkindly suggested the buses could tow the prams behind them. When the final journey came on 25th September 1930, car no 17 was used. This was the same car which made the first trip when the line was first electrified in July 1905.

During 1931 local inhabitants were surprised to see a trolleybus operating experimentally between Yarmouth and Caister. It was a Garrett single-deck vehicle which for the occasion used one trolley on the overhead wire with the earth return being a 'skate' trailing along behind in the tramway rail. This unusual practice had previously been used on a regular basis in Birmingham where trolleybuses had to use tram-only routes to reach the depot. There

Services between Haven Bridge and Gorleston began on 4th July 1905 although the bridge was never crossed and the town's tramway remained in two parts throughout. A car passes the Quay making for Gorleston Beach c1910. (Lens of Sutton)

The Quay at Gorleston in September 1990. The route between Southtown and Gorleston closed in September 1930 after only 25 years of service although trams survived on the northern section to Caister until December 1933. (Author)

the skate resembled and acquired the nickname of 'a string of sausages'. At Yarmouth it was thought that the corporation might proceed with trolleybuses but the idea never materialised.

As the number of motor buses increased so the end of the tramway system came nearer. It survived until 14th December 1933 when car no 6 made the final journey from the market place to the depot. The car was driven by Mayor Peter Ellis, the conductor was Alderman Arthur Beevor and other council members were passengers. Many onlookers were present and to mark the occasion fog detonators exploded on the track. After tea in the mess room, the Chairman of the Transport Committee made a closing speech during which he said had Shakespeare been present he might have said:

'Farewell, old tram, no more can you be mended;
   Go rest in peace
Your useful life has ended.'

Many of the cars finished their lives as holiday chalets at a Caister holiday camp and it was not long before most of the rails had gone. The tracks at the Caister Road depot were covered not long ago and the depot now serves Great Yarmouth Transport buses. Above the depot entrance can be seen effigies of the various stages of travel – the Rocket, a coach and a bus. At Gorleston the past is remembered by the Tramway Inn with a signboard showing a Great Yarmouth tram. The site of the old horsetram depot that once stood nearby is today occupied by the public library.

Recollections of the past still continue to be found. At the East Anglia Transport Museum at Carlton Colville there is a pre-First World War junction box which had earlier stood in the town's streets in its heavy cast iron cabinet. Also towards the end of October 1989 the *Great Yarmouth Mercury* reported that whilst digging along Caister Road, workmen unearthed fragments of old tramlines beneath the road – a recollection of the system that was abandoned some 56 years previously.

Chapter 7

TRAMS PRESERVED AT CARLTON COLVILLE

(East Anglia Transport Museum)

How could anyone thinking themselves any sort of transport enthusiast ever contemplate visiting East Anglia without paying a visit to the East Anglia Transport Museum (EATM)! Situated at Carlton Colville not far from Lowestoft, it can be found just off the Beccles – Lowestoft road (A146) along Chapel Road (B1384). Open from Easter to the end of September on Sundays and Bank Holidays (plus Saturdays from June to September), also on week-days during August, it exhibits a wide range of trams and trolleybuses plus many preserved road vehicles from motor cars to steam rollers and a narrow gauge railway.

The museum was founded on its present site in 1965 when a small band of local enthusiasts was reorganised to become the East Anglia Transport Museum Society. The museum started with just a few vehicles which had already been donated or loaned but there were no other assets. The society faced the task of transforming disused meadows – kindly provided by the society's founder and first chairman, Mr A V Bird – into a museum and all that it entails. Workshops and offices were needed as well as stores, refreshment facilities, toilets and so forth. In addition, if running trams or trolleybuses were ever to be contemplated, then roads, tracks and overhead wires were needed.

The museum has throughout its life been brought together entirely by amateurs with finance coming mostly from enthusiasts

The only known tram with gutters and a downspout . . . The body of this 1904 single-deck Lowestoft tram spent 60 years built into the back of a bungalow in Lowestoft before being acquired by the East Anglia Transport Museum in January 1990. In the medium term it will serve as a stationary exhibit. (Author)

plus money spent or donated by visitors. In addition the majority of the work is carried out by members who give their time completely free of charge. It is to their credit therefore that by the end of 1966 the first buildings were erected with the first road construction and tram track completed the same year. On 12th November 1970 development was sufficiently well advanced for a tramcar, Blackpool 159, to be operated under its own power for the first time at Carlton Colville. Not long afterwards a London Transport trolleybus made history by being the first to be worked in a museum anywhere in the country.

There was great excitement when, on 24th May 1972, the museum opened to the public. In the same year a narrow gauge railway was constructed in time to commence at Whitsun 1973. It had really become a place for a day out – for all the family. The not-so-young could rekindle memories with the trams and trolleybuses on exhibition and the young could look on in wonder at these strange vehicles of the past. New amenities were gradually added and surely enthusiasts dreams were realised when, from July 1982, they could take an extended tram ride through woodland to a new terminus at Hedley Grove.

The well known preserved 'Diddler' trolleybus at Carlton Colville on 23rd September 1990, its last day before leaving the museum having been on loan from the London Transport Museum, Covent Garden. The Diddler, built in 1931 served initially on the London United Tramways routes around Kingston in Surrey. (Author)

Trams exhibited range from the early open-top double-decker to the sturdier large-capacity city tramcar. An early vehicle is Lowestoft car no 14 superbly restored from the many years it spent as a summerhouse before being 'rescued' in 1961. The car was built by Milnes in 1904 for the Lowestoft Corporation where it survived until replaced by buses in 1931. It is typical of many trams constructed for use throughout the country early this century. It was originally built for a 3 ft 6 ins gauge although its present truck is standard gauge to permit movement on museum track.

Another vehicle relevant to the Eastern Counties is the Ransomes, Sims and Jefferies trolleybus no 44 (DX 8871) which dates

from 1930 (see chapter 4). This trackless 'tram' was built for Ipswich Corporation and in 1955 it was presented to the Clapham Transport Museum. It joined the Carlton Colville exhibits in 1974. The popularity of the trolleybus was at its highest during the 1930s when it was seen as a more flexible replacement for the tram but still retaining some of the tram's better features. Yet they were comparatively short-lived since after 1950 the high cost of electricity and the maintenance of the overhead wiring helped to bring about their decline, at a time of cheaply imported crude oil.

There is much more to see at Carlton Colville. Walking the museum's roadway with its tram tracks seems like a trip back into the past with items such as Victorian pillar boxes, ornate street lighting columns and road signs, horse troughs and drinking fountains, a shop window displaying many items of yesteryear, plus an example of the first type of public telephone kiosk – complete with 'buttons A and B'. Three tramway junction boxes are to be found having previously been used as street-side equipment – one was formerly used by Great Yarmouth Corporation Tramways.

London HR/2 tram 1858 passes admiring spectators at Carlton Colville. Built by English Electric in 1930 for use on hilly routes in the capital, it was purchased for preservation in 1952. Prior to its arrival at Carlton Colville, it spent a number of years at Chessington Zoo as a static exhibit. (Roy Makewell)

This Sunbeam MF2B Weymann-bodied trolleybus served in Bournemouth until 1968. It was later 'rescued' from a scrap merchant for preservation. It is photographed here in the late 1970s. (East Anglia Transport Museum)

One of the latest exhibits at the museum is the body of a single-deck tram from the Lowestoft system. Only four of this type were ever operated in East Anglia, all of them being in Lowestoft (see chapter 5). This tram, which ran in service from 1904 to 1930, will eventually be painted in the old Lowestoft livery and utilised for the display of small objects.

In addition the author found tucked away behind the terminus of the 2 ft gauge light railway the rather worse-for-wear body of a Norwich tram. This was a rebuilt car, numbered 39, and a replacement of Norwich's original no 39. Its future at the museum is uncertain and, by the time this book is published, it may have moved on elsewhere. The original no 39 is ending its days in a private garden at Sprowston, north of Norwich, but it is not accessible to the public.

23rd September 1990 proved to be a special day at the East Anglia Transport Museum since it bade farewell to a famous visitor. This was the 'Diddler', London's trolleybus no 1, which had been on loan from the London Transport Museum at Covent Garden. The 'Diddler' was the trolleybus version of London's streamlined 'Feltham' tramcar of 1931. During the day it was possible to ride in the nearly 60 years old 'Diddler' – a special event indeed. In addition the author was able to travel on two other trolleybuses, one from Maidstone and another from London as well as a London 'HR/2' and a Blackpool standard tram. What more could one ask for on a day out with so many exhibits and no problem to park the car!!

Chapter 8

CROSS CITY SERVICES IN A COUNTY TOWN

(Norwich Electric Tramways Company)

The City of Norwich covers approximately 15½ square miles but fortunately for the visitor much of its charm is confined to an area of less than two square miles. Its well known castle and cathedral date back to Norman times and its medieval Guildhall was built 80 years before Columbus discovered America!

Inevitably Norwich has many museums. One of these is the Mustard Shop in Bridewell Alley where visitors can recall the past in evocative surroundings. Colmans first began making 'Penny Oval' tins of mustard in 1886 when quantities of either 12 or 13 drams of fine mustard were sold – dependent upon how well the company was doing. It seems that last century a penny (less than ½p) went a long way. In 1899 Mr E B Southwell, a former manager and director of J & J Colman Ltd said, 'The Penny Tin pays everybody. The penny pays the farmer who grows the seed, the railway company, the cost of manufacture, making the tin, printing the label, weighing and filling, despatching, the wholesaler's profit, the grocer's profit, and everybody is satisfied –

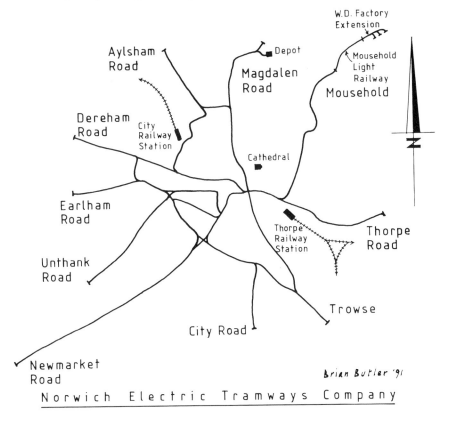

Brian Butler '91

Norwich   Electric   Tramways   Company

Car no 38 passes St Giles church c1906. The buildings have long since gone and the area is now a roundabout and dual carriageway. (Lens of Sutton)

including the customer who gets a supply of excellent mustard for his humble penny'.

Only a few doors away is the Bridewell Museum of Norwich Trade and Industries. Exhibits range from a colourful textiles display to the splendour of a steam fire engine. The scale model of a tram is also prominently displayed. This was made by the late Russell Gamble of Norwich c1960 and donated to the museum by Mrs P Gamble in 1987. This superb exhibit complete with traction poles and overhead wire is of car no 35 with its destination board reading 'Earlham Road and Thorpe Road'. The museum's other tramway exhibits include numerous tickets, badges and buttons, a tram driver's cap, a destination board, portfolio plans for the city dating from the 1890s and a 3 ft section of rail recovered from St Andrew Street.

The first public transport system in Norwich comprised a horse drawn bus service provided by the Norwich Omnibus Company Ltd which began between Thorpe railway station and Dereham Road on 23rd June 1879. Other routes ran from Newmarket Road to Catton at the Whalebone public house, Unthank Road to Bracondale and from Earlham Road to Thorpe Village. The vehicles were single-deckers with the driver's seat high up. The driver collected the fares through a trap door set in the roof. On the route from Thorpe station to Thorpe Gardens, double-deckers were used with knifeboard seating on top.

Prior to the buses there had been applications for tramway systems but these had not materialised. In 1883 a cable tramway was proposed by Andrew Hallidie, an American from San Francisco. The idea was that a cable running in a conduit between the rails would be attached to a car by a controllable gripper with the cable wound on and off a drum at the cable station. The scheme was considered by the Norwich City Council's Parliamentary and By-Laws Committee which considered the construction and working of the system would cause considerable 'nuisance and discomfort'. Accordingly the company gave up its proposal although it is worth noting that Hallidie's cable trams still operate in San Francisco even though mainly as a tourist attraction.

Two further schemes came and went. In 1886 the Norwich Tramways Company Ltd came into existence and a Tramways Order was granted the following year. Despite this, the company gave up the idea in December 1889. Seven years later in 1896 the British Electric Traction Company (BET) proposed a company to be known as the Norwich and District Light Railways which would build a network of light railways to connect as far afield as Hingham to the west and Bungay and Beccles to the south east. However this was not to be and it was the Norwich Electric Tramways Company, incorporated by the New General Traction Company, that finally gained the City Council's consent. A Bill was approved by Parliament on 20th July 1897 and in February 1898 the City Council gave the go-ahead for work to commence.

Considerable street improvements were necessary before the tracks could be laid. There were many narrow streets, numerous curves and some steep gradients with the steepest at 1 in 14.5. Certain streets had to be widened and a new street had to be cut on St Andrews Hill through the buildings in Redwell Street. An ironmongers shop on Orford Hill had to be demolished. There was much hard bargaining over the various construction costs and it was eventually agreed that this should be shared between the company and the council. As far as the company was concerned, this was in addition to its expected responsibility under the 1870 Tramways Act to repair the tramway and the roadway between the rails and 18 inches on each side. The gauge was 3 ft 6 ins and over 15 route miles were built. Overhead wires were used for the 550v DC current collection. The current for the overhead wires came from a two-storey brick power station in Duke Street constructed by the tramway company. The depot and repair shops were sited in Silver Street where all 50 cars could be accommodated.

Just over three years after Parliamentary approval, the grand opening came. On 30th July 1900 the electric trams commenced services on four routes in the city. Crowds lined the streets to watch and it is said that men being shaved left their chairs with

Car no 11 on the Thorpe Road and Newmarket Road service passes the Fountain c1906 which was situated at the junction of Newmarket Road and Ipswich Road. (Colin Withey collection)

Cars 40 and 16 pass at the Royal Hotel end of Castle Meadow with the picture looking down Prince of Wales Road. Car no 16 was one of five sold to Coventry in 1910. (Lens of Sutton)

Looking down Prince of Wales Road, September 1990. Not much has changed except that the building on the right now houses Anglia Television. (Author)

lather on their faces to stand and stare at the trams as they 'clanged and swished' past them. The success of the trams was undoubted. Routes included Magdalen Road, Earlham Road, Dereham Road and Thorpe Road. Other routes opened later that year included Aylsham Road, Mousehold Heath, Newmarket Road, City Road and Trowse. By the end of the year a further route opened along Unthank Road. At first all services operated to and from the Tramway Centre at Orford Place with its circular waiting room. The centre soon became very congested so that from April 1901 cross-city services were introduced on most routes. In 1904 the track at Orford Place was relaid thus further easing the situation.

The initial fleet consisted of 50 cars comprising 40 motor cars and 10 trailer cars. They were all double-deck open-top four-wheel cars mounted on Peckham Cantilever trucks with 30 inch diameter wheels. Most of the cars were equipped with two West-inghouse 25 hp motors although a number had 30 hp motors. The bodies, built by the Brush Electrical Engineering Company had seating for 52 passengers with an equal number inside or on top. Inside the seats were longitudinal with rugs for upholstery whereas on top garden-type seats with covers were used. The livery was maroon and ivory and the trailer cars were used mostly on the service to Trowse and to Mousehold when traffic was heavy.

Life was hard for the staff at such times. A conductor was paid 3d (just over 1p) an hour but a motorman did better at 4d (just over 1½p) an hour. Services on all routes started between 6.30 am and 7 am but with a later start on Sundays. There was no guaranteed week and there were no holidays. Rules were strict with conditions laid down. Any crews backing a car without reversing the trolley rendered themselves liable to dismissal. Dogs were not allowed on the cars except for small dogs held on laps.

Norwich's tramways had a rather unusual ticket issuing system. The conductor had a cylindrical canister (about the size of the one pound cocoa tin of the day) painted black and containing a spool on which he slid rolls of tickets. Each roll was separated by a circular piece of cardboard and the tickets projected through a slot in the canister. They were torn off as required and then punched by a hand machine to cancel and also register the number issued. It was a system used in Coventry where the tramway company was also a New General Traction Company subsidiary.

In 1909 Norwich was visited by King Edward VII when a Royal Conferment ceremony was held in St Andrew's Hall. It was an occasion when His Majesty bestowed upon Dr Ernest E Blyth and his successors the Honour and Title of Lord Mayor. The City of Norwich as the chief City of East Anglia had always enjoyed a close relationship with His Majesty. It was also an occasion when the City's trams found a new role. Apart from catering for the very heavy traffic, numerous cars were positioned at various vantage points and used as grandstands. Charges were made at 1/- (5p) on top and 6d (2½p) inside.

Two years later in 1911, the ten trailer cars were withdrawn since they had not proved a success. Five of them (43–47) were

A tram passes the market at Gentleman's Walk c1919. The car is on the Unthank Road to Magdalen Road route. After the First World War further routes were constructed via Queen Street to reach the 'Cricketers Arms' at City Road and Trowse. (Pamlin Prints)

motorised and they worked the route from Aylsham Road to Trowse. In 1914, just prior to the First World War, the tramway company obtained powers to construct a number of additional routes but the outset of hostilities meant they had to be abandoned. Not only were metals in short supply but coal was also short and manpower was reduced. As the war progressed services were curtailed and many late journeys were stopped.

Near the end of the war the War Department established an aerodrome and armaments factory to the northeast of the city just beyond Mousehold Heath. Since transport to the site for materials was necessary, the War Department asked the Norwich Electric Tramways Company if it could help. The company agreed to build a light railway to the factory but the necessary materials were at that time not available. The problem was solved when rails in King Street were lifted following the cutting back of the Aylsham Road to Trowse route to the Royal Hotel leaving Trowse isolated. A single track covering just over ½ mile was laid across the Heath using the King Street rails laid on wooden sleepers. At the factory several sidings radiated from a loop beyond which a small steam locomotive was used.

Two freight motors, Government-owned, were built by the tramway company and used to haul flat cars, providing a link between the aerodrome and Thorpe railway station. At the station a single track spur ran to the railway sidings where transhipment could take place. After the war the freight motors passed to the tramway company which in 1923 used the units to build new cars (part of the rolling stock renewal programme of 1924/1925) but the track was not lifted until the 1930s when the tramway system closed.

After the war, using the 1914 powers, the service to Trowse was restored but now via Queen's Road and Bracondale. A branch from the route reached the Cricketers Arms at City Road. There was criticism over the infrequent service on these routes. It is said that a commercial traveller came out of a shop in Queen's Road

This building, photographed in September 1990 at the junction of Silver Road and Sprowston Road, was the Norwich tramway company's general office from 1926 until closure. The office was previously situated on Timber Hill. (Author)

anxious to reach the city as soon as possible. He asked an elderly gentleman with a long white beard who was sitting on a public seat on St Catherine's Plain if he had recently seen a tram bound for the city. The old gentleman replied with dry humour, 'I was a boy when the last tram passed here'.

The tramway company was proud of its freedom from serious accidents. Often trams had run off their lines but without any serious injury to passengers. Yet two serious incidents were recorded. Around 1925 an Unthank Road tram ran off the rails and crashed into a wall near St Giles' Gate. At about the same time two Dereham Road trams collided head-on in thick fog near Nelson Street, one of the drivers being injured. There were two other incidents both involving men who insisted on standing on the open top deck. Both were injured when they fell into the road but not seriously.

In April 1925 the tram routes from the Aylsham Road terminus to the Royal Hotel and the branch via City station were closed and replaced by buses. On 24th March 1930 the route from Orford Place to City Road ceased operation. In the same year a special committee appointed by the City Council to consider passenger transport in Norwich recommended that the corporation should seek powers to provide a municipal bus service. It also considered that trams were 'a source of congestion in the streets of the city' and no extensions to the present system were desirable. Purchase of the tramways by the corporation, it claimed, was 'not a practical proposition on the basis laid down in the Tramways Act'.

In the original 1897 Norwich Electric Tramways Act, it was stipulated that the undertaking could be purchased 35 years after the date of the Act and thereafter at intervals of seven years. This meant that such powers could be exercised in 1932. The City Council was anxious to go ahead with purchase although a number of members were against the idea. On 30th November 1932 Norwich Corporation promoted a Bill to authorise purchase of the tramway with a view to abandoning the system and substituting buses. A public meeting was held when the proposal was rejected by 314 votes to 275.

There were strong feelings in the city for and against purchase of the tramway company by the corporation and a Tramway Opposition Committee was formed. In the end the City Council organised a poll of citizens over the controversy and this was arranged for 10th January 1933. The opposition committee lost no time in informing residents the costs that would be involved and how the ratepayers would be affected. Some 90,000 leaflets were distributed and sandwich-men carrying appropriate placards paraded the streets. The result of the poll showed 11,033 against the purchase and 7,775 for purchase. Despite all the publicity only 29 per cent turned out to vote.

Almost a year later, in December 1933, it was announced that the Eastern Counties Omnibus Company Limited had acquired a controlling interest in the tramway company. It therefore became

The body of Norwich tramcar no 39 photographed at the East Anglia Transport Museum at Carlton Colville on 23rd September 1990. Originally a Brush car, it was one of 34 vehicles which were rebuilt with English Electric bodies in December 1924. (Author)

inevitable that within a few weeks, the omnibus company announced its intention to abandon the trams in favour of buses. Yet the trams were far from dead since during 1934 over ll million passengers were carried compared with over 7 million by motor bus. The abandonment Bill finally received Royal Assent on 6th June 1935 after which time buses gradually took over the various routes.

The last tram (car no 10) ran on 10th December 1935 when it left Orford Place for Eaton and then back to the tram sheds at Silver Road. It left just after 11 pm to the accompaniment of cheering crowds and the tram was packed with passengers. One of these was Mr Charles Watling, ex-Sheriff of Norwich who had also ridden on the city's first tram. According to the *Eastern Daily Press* of 11th December 1935, when the tram reached the Eaton terminus the passengers sang 'Auld Lang Syne' for the twelfth time. Its last journey to the depot was 'to a fantasia of cheers and bell-ringing' with a long trail of cycles and cars following behind. At the sheds the crowds joined hands round the car and sang 'Auld Lang Syne' for, it was claimed, the 36th time!

After closure tramcar bodies minus their trucks and glass were available for purchase at £5 each. Yet two of these are known to have survived. One was discovered at Sprowston but it is in a private garden and is not accessible. The other is at the East Anglia Transport Museum at Carlton Colville but in a rather sorry state. It was a Brush car and was one of 34 vehicles which was rebuilt with an English Electric body in December 1924.

Orford Place, once a tramway centre, is today a pedestrianised area. It was narrowed following rebuilding after bombing during the Second World War. The tramway company's offices, initially on Timber Hill, moved in 1926 to a building in Silver Road adjoining the tram depot. The tram depot today has gone, the site now an estate of houses known as Bellingham Court. The office building is still there close to the junction between Silver Road and Sprowston Road. The name of the tramway company has been removed from the facade abutting the roof but it is still possible to see where it was written .

Chapter 9

TRAMS DRIVEN BY STEAM

(The Wolverton & Stony Stratford Tramway, the Wisbech &
Upwell Tramway and the Alford & Sutton Tramway)

The Wolverton & Stony Stratford Tramway

Wolverton owes its existence largely to the fact that the London &
Birmingham Railway Company chose it as a site for a new railway
works. Sheds and workshops were opened in 1838 and the company also constructed houses, schools and a church for its employees. Before the railway came, the village of Wolverton had only
about 500 inhabitants and the station was opened there primarily
to serve Stony Stratford just over two miles to the west. The latter
had a population of around 1,750 with many of the female population engaged in the manufacture of lace.

Transport between the two towns was sparse indeed with only a
number of small horse buses making the journey. One, owned by
Mr Rich, could carry only four passengers inside and two outside.
Another 'bus', owned by Joseph Clare who was landlord at the
Cock Inn in the High Street, could accommodate just two inside
and two outside. Only a few doors away from the Cock Inn was the
Bull Inn owned by Thomas Carter and there was much rivalry
between the two landlords. Both became well known for their tall
stories and it has been said this is how the expression 'a Cock and
Bull story' originated.

Later the railway (known as the London & North Western
Railway – LNWR – from 16th July 1846) took its locomotive works

*Wolverton & Stony
Stratford's Green tram
no 1 about to haul two
100-seater cars c1910.
The sag in the cars
through heavy loads is
already beginning to show.
(Lens of Sutton)*

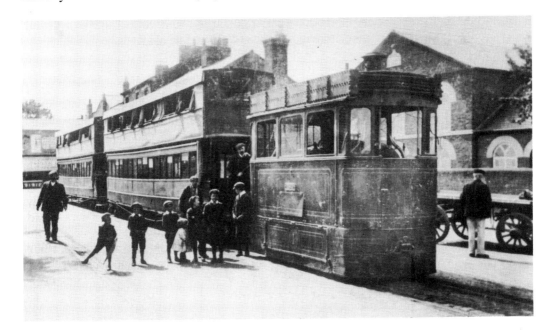

Bagnall no 5 and a 100-seater car at the Foresters Arms awaiting departure to Wolverton. Note the bogies placed at the extreme end of the car so that the couplings remained central over the track when negotiating curves. (Lens of Sutton)

to Crewe and the Wolverton works concentrated on carriage building requiring yet more employees. This, combined with the arrival in 1878 of McCorquodale & Company, the large printing and stationery works, meant that adequate transport in the area had become an urgent necessity. McCorquodale's business was very transport orientated and rivalled the Bell Punch Company in the production of tickets for tramways as well as railways.

First attempts to produce a light railway came in November 1882 when the Wolverton & Stony Stratford Tramways Co Ltd was formed by local interests. It was not successful and in less than a year it was placed in voluntary liquidation. However one of its few corporate acts granted the registration of a new company with a similar name, so on 6th September 1883 the Wolverton & Stony Stratford & District Tramway Co Ltd was formed. Meantime a Tramways Order had been promoted by Frederick Charles Winby, a civil engineer and contractor. This had been granted on 16th July 1883 authorising 2 miles 54 chains of single track, 4 ft gauge, between the towns. When incorporated, the new company acquired Winby's rights and interests in the Order. Winby undertook to build the line but, like the previous attempt, the endeavour fell through.

Eventually in August 1886 serious progress was made. Charles Herbert Wilkinson of Wilkinson & Co, a local firm of contractors, had already shown interest in a number of schemes including one to link Newport Pagnell and Olney and on 18th August 1886 he agreed a contract to built the Wolverton line for £13,325. The name of the company was changed to the Wolverton, Stony Stratford & District Light Railways Co Ltd. The shares offered for sale were quickly taken up and so work began.

Board of Trade sanction for services to commence was given on 20th May 1887. The line was mostly single and it was built to the 3 ft 6 in gauge and not the 4 ft gauge originally authorised. Public passenger traffic began a week later on 27th May between the Barley Mow Inn at Stony Stratford and Wolverton railway station to connect with all up and down trains and at times required by the local workers. Initially two steam tram-engines supplied by Krauss of Munich hauled large covered-top double-deck passenger cars obtained from the Midland Carriage and Wagon Co of Shrewsbury.

Two months after opening, an extension of 2 miles 3 chains from Stony Stratford's High Street to Deanshanger was agreed. Work went ahead immediately and a line running almost parallel to the Grand Junction Canal opened later that year. It was hoped the extension, a private scheme of Wilkinson's which he leased to the company, would encourage considerable freight traffic from the Britannia Ironworks of E & H Roberts at Deanshanger and in anticipation Wilkinson acquired another Krauss tram-engine plus numerous freight wagons. Two of the wagons were somewhat versatile since they were made with retractable flanges which also allowed road haulage by horses where no track existed. A small 4-wheeled car was also purchased to cater for occasional passenger traffic. Unhappily for Wilkinson freight traffic on the extension was not forthcoming since the ironworks kept its trade with the canal carriers who had previously brought in considerable business.

In March 1888 a contract was agreed with the LNWR for delivery of goods traffic. Despite this by mid-1889 the company ran into serious financial problems and on 4th September it declared itself insolvent and went into voluntary liquidation. This was contested by various creditors but a Court Order on 26th October closed the line. For about two years the local people had no trams and it was not until 1891 that a local benefactor, Herbert Samuel Leon, of Bletchley Park joined with the local Field family to rescue the company. After negotiations with the Receiver, a public service was reinstated on 20th November 1891. This was a purely private arrangement which lasted until September 1893 when yet another tramway company with an even longer title, the Wolverton and Stony Stratford and District New Tramway Company Limited, was formed and controlled by the Leon and Field families.

A Bagnall saddle-tank engine hauls two 100-seater workmen's cars in LNWR livery along a country section of the Wolverton-Stony Stratford route in the early 1920s. (Lens of Sutton)

The Deanshanger extension was no longer in use and the Stony Stratford terminus was cut back to the Cock Inn. The carriage of freight was confined mainly to LNWR parcel traffic and the handling of mail for the Postmaster General. A small store building to handle parcel traffic was established near the gate of the depot at Stony Stratford and also a small office and waiting room opened at the corner of High Street and Wolverton Road next door to the Foresters Arms. By this time the earlier Krauss tram-engines had been replaced by engines from T Green & Sons with the Krauss no 3 kept as stand-by.

In 1900 a further tram-engine was purchased from the Brush Electrical Company but it was hardly a satisfactory acquisition. Its cylinders were smaller than the Krauss engines and it could just about haul a workmen's tram. It continually broke down necessitating expensive and difficult repairs. It was perhaps the passenger cars that aroused the most interest. To carry the workers there were three large double-deck cars each on two 4-wheel bogies and each capable of seating 100 passengers. The cars were 44 ft long and each had as many as 16 windows on either side. Interior illumination after dark was from oil-lamps although these were later replaced by the LNWR for acetylene lights. Further cars available carried fewer numbers and these were generally used for passengers other than workpeople. In later years a problem with the larger cars was that they acquired a visible sag at the centre because of the heavy loads carried although the cars were subsequently overhauled.

In 1910 economies and increasing motor traffic caused the High Street section to be abandoned and cars found a new terminus outside the Foresters Arms in the Wolverton Road. Not surprisingly the presence of 44 ft long cars created problems for other vehicles especially when in train formation. The trams received their first direct competition in 1914 when motor buses from Bedford extended their service to Stony Stratford. Relief came for the trams, however, when war was declared and the whole of the Bedford fleet was requisitioned by the War Office. As the war progressed so maintenance of the tramway system became more difficult. Costs outstripped revenue and in 1916 a motorbus was introduced to help maintain a regular timetable. By the end of the war in 1918 the condition of the tramway was described as 'little better than derelict'.

As a result the company went into liquidation on 17th July 1919 and matters were worsened when the local authorities refused to become involved. Since 700 workers were still being carried daily, the LNWR stepped in and at the end of 1919 purchased the entire undertaking – a move it was soon to regret. A small saddle-tank locomotive was purchased from W & G Bagnall & Co and the tramway was completely re-laid with concrete placed beneath the rails. Meantime by the spring of 1920 motor buses from Bedford were providing a half-hourly service through Stony Stratford and the trams, with their 8 mph speed limit, continued to lose money.

The London, Midland & Scottish Railway Company, which took over the LNWR in 1923, struggled on and soon the trams were almost deserted. The General Strike came in 1926 and on 4th May services were suspended never to be resumed.

Numerous items from the Wolverton & Stony Stratford Tramway can be seen today at the Milton Keynes Museum of Industry and Rural Life in Wolverton (open between Easter and the end of October, Wednesday to Sunday). Transport is a strong theme at the museum with exhibits ranging from tram tickets to parts of the original tramcars. The bottom half of no 5 tramcar has been preserved as well as the top and bottom half of a smaller car although, as might be expected, they are in poor condition. In addition copies of original drawings from Wolverton Works are still in existence. Iron track measures and some tramcar seats can also be found plus part of the original track which is displayed in setts as it would have been when originally in use.

Wisbech & Upwell Tramway

Constructed as a Great Eastern Railway (GER) venture, the tramway that eventually linked Wisbech with Upwell was mainly built to assist agriculture in the area. An earlier proposal for such a line had come from a man called Gillard who had obtained powers but due to financial problems the idea was abandoned. During 1878/1880, the GER was experimenting with its Kitson steam tram engine no 230 on the Millwall Extension Railway on London's Isle of Dogs. In 1880 the GER resurrected the Upwell scheme by proposing a tramway to be worked by steam locomotives, but within the provisions of the Tramways Act of 1870 to cut costs.

An Act was agreed by Parliament on 24th July 1882 and construction began at once. On 20th August 1883 the tramway

Staff pose beside steam locomotives nos 136 and 135 on the Wisbech – Upwell Tramway. These locomotives were built in 1903. Some of these engines were later used on quayside lines at Yarmouth and Ipswich. (Lens of Sutton)

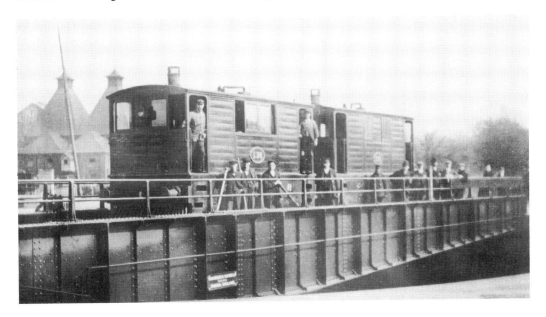

A steam train travels alongside the Wisbech–Upwell Canal of 1794. The tramway closed to passengers on 2nd January 1928 but survived for freight until 23rd May 1966. (Lens of Sutton)

opened from Wisbech (GER station) to Outwell. It is recorded that, soon after opening, some 3,000 passengers were being carried each week in addition to around 600 tons of goods. The extension from Outwell to Upwell followed on 8th September 1884 giving an overall distance of almost six miles. The standard gauge track followed the bank of the former Wisbech Canal of 1794, much of it parallel to the A1101 roadway. In places the track was laid in the roadway, embedded in the surface so as not to obstruct road vehicles. Initially this was done with cinder ballast although in later years stones were used covered with tarmacadam.

The original tram locomotives were designed by Thomas Worsdell (GER Locomotive Superintendent 1881-1885) being 0-4-0 tanks. They had cow-catchers, warning bells and governors which shut off steam and applied brakes should 12 mph be exceeded. Enclosed in wooden casing, they had more the appearance of a railway freight brake van. Some of these survived grouping to become LNER class Y6. Between 1903 and 1921 a number of the locomotives were replaced by more powerful 0-6-0T fully enclosed locomotives (GER class C53 – LNER class J70) designed by Holden (GER Locomotive Superintendent 1885–1907).

For the first year of operation four-wheeled carriages only were

The Wisbech & Upwell Tramway c1910. The 0-4-0 tram locomotives were fitted with cow catchers and warning bells and were enclosed in wooden casing giving more the appearance of a freight brake van. (Lens of Sutton)

used. Manufactured by Starbuck about 1870/1871, these were ex-horse trams which came from the Millwall Extension Railway. In 1884 bogie coaches were introduced. These had end platforms with ornamental railings and were provided with steps since the stations lacked platforms. When passenger services ceased in 1928, six coaches were transferred to the Kelvedon & Tollesbury Light Railway and one of these (no 8) was later used for the filming in 1953 of The Titfield Thunderbolt on a section of disused track near Camerton in Avon. Tragically it was scrapped by British Rail. In 1913 a further car went to the Elsenham & Thaxted line. During much of the Wisbech & Upwell Tramway's life there were eight trams daily and as far as freight was concerned over 500 tons of produce was carried in the year 1888. Goods traffic varied according to season yet during the year 1910 as much as 14,549 tons was achieved.

Alford & Sutton Tramway's steam locomotive no 1 with its vertical boiler was built in 1883 by Black, Hawthorn & Co of Gateshead under a Wilkinson patent. The picture was probably taken prior to the line's opening in April 1884 when used as a contractor's tram during construction of the line. (Lens of Sutton)

Passenger services on the tramway ceased with the final journey on 1st January 1928 because of increasing competition from the roads although freight traffic continued. Towards the end, working was by specially equipped BR Drewry diesel locomotives but traffic continued to decrease. In 1961 the British Transport Commission announced that the line would close but such was the reaction from local fruit growers that the date was postponed.

The tramway survived a further five years but finally on 23rd May 1966 the end came. The last goods tram made its way along the track three days earlier, accompanied by a convoy of cars. Three enthusiasts even managed to get a ride aboard the three trucks and guards van. *The Eastern Daily Press* commented, 'No one could have described this as a memorable funeral for the 83-year old line, the last link of its kind in the country. The occasion seemed to give the curious, rather than the genuinely sad, an excuse for an afternoon out. The Wisbech-Upwell tramway went out of operation quietly and even a little ignominiously'.

Happily for posterity, the body of one Wisbech & Upwell tramcar is still in existence. Car no 7, a bogie composite coach, was one of those transferred to the Kelvedon & Tollesbury Light Railway but, after this line closed in 1951, the car suffered the indignity of serving for over 20 years as an onion store on a farm near Ramsey. After 'rescue' in 1973, it was for a time with the Cambridge Museum of Technology but in July 1982 it was moved to the Rutland Railway Museum, Cottesmore, near Oakham in Leicestershire. The car returned to Wisbech on 20th August 1983 during celebrations to mark one hundred years since the line opened – its first return visit to Wisbech for well over 50 years! The body today is in poor condition although the framework is fair. Unfortunately both balconies were removed to facilitate earlier transit. Yet there are hopes that the Rutland Railway Museum, given adequate finance and labour, might have the car working by the late 1990s.

The Alford & Sutton Tramway

If visiting the Louth area of Lincolnshire then travel along the A157 Mablethorpe road and find the Legbourne Railway Museum (open March to September, Tuesday to Sunday) at Britain's oldest preserved Great Northern Railway (GNR) station. Rail services first commenced at Legbourne Road in 1848 being the first section of the GNR to open to fare paying passengers. After complete closure of the line in 1970, the station was later restored to become a typical country station as it would have looked in later LNER days.

Yet apart from the station and the many items of memorabilia collected over the years by Mike and Sheila Legge, one item is of considerable interest to tram enthusiasts. This is the signal box that was once in use at the nearby Alford & Sutton Tramway which closed over a century ago, in December 1889. For many years the box stood in a field at Sutton-on-Sea where a farmer used it as a hen house, allowing it to considerably deteriorate. Now restored at Legbourne, a nine lever frame has been installed (from a box at Claxby near Market Rasen on the Great Central line) plus a block shelf with a selection of instruments. One board on the side of the box reads 'Legbourne Road' and the other (not original boards) 'Tramway Crossing' as a recollection from its Alford & Sutton Tramway days.

During the 1870s rail traffic reached the small seaside towns of Mablethorpe (from Louth) and Skegness (from Firsby). The towns grew rapidly in popularity and many excursions were made from London and the surrounding counties. During the year 1878 alone as many as 200,000 holiday-makers travelled to Skegness. However, the Sutton-on-Sea area was still without trains and it therefore followed that transport to the coast should be considered.

74

Accordingly plans were deposited in 1880 for a 2 ft 6 ins gauge steam tramway between Alford (on the East Lincolnshire line from Louth to Firsby) and Sutton-le-Marsh (as it was known) serving the villages of Bilsby, Markby and Hannah. The Act was passed in August 1880 for trams to run along the public highway to carry goods, minerals and other traffic in addition to passengers. During construction a further Act was passed in 1883 for a second tramway to run from Skegness via Hogsthorpe and Mumby to join the Alford and Sutton Tramway at Bilsby but this never developed. In any event there would have been problems for at a later stage there were attempts to build this second line at the standard 4 ft 8½ ins gauge which would have made a junction at Bilsby impractical.

There were delays before work could start between Alford and Sutton and because of this a further Bill was passed on August 10th 1882 agreeing an extension of time. Construction eventually

The signal box which stood at Tramway Crossing at Sutton-on-Sea today resides at the Legbourne Railway Museum to the south of Louth. For many years the box had remained at its original site used by a farmer for his chickens! (Picture: Mike Legge)

started on 14th December 1882 undertaken by a Scottish firm called W B Dick & Co, the principal of which, Mr Dick, owned the tramway. At Alford, close to Alford Town railway station, Argyle House was built to serve as a tramway office and behind were erected workshops and rolling stock storage sheds. A smaller shed was built at Sutton. Along the route there were several occasions where the roadway had to be raised or lowered to ease the gradients.

Finally on 2nd April 1884 the line opened and the inhabitants of Alford decided to celebrate. According to the *Lincoln Gazette* the main street from the railway station to the town centre was decorated with flags, bunting and Venetian masts painted red, white and blue. All the shops were closed during the afternoon so that the maximum number of people could try out the new transport. Large numbers of people turned out and goods wagons as well as carriages had to be used in order to carry them! During the evening a public tea-party was held at the Corn Exchange which was well attended. At the public meeting which followed, after the Queen and the Armed Forces and others had been toasted, the chairman proposed success to the tramway. In his reply, Mr Dick added caution by stating he believed the undertaking would succeed but 'it may be necessary to wait a year or so'.

During its life the tramway possessed only three engines. No 1 with a vertical boiler was built in 1883 by Black, Hawthorn & Co of Gateshead under a Wilkinson patent whereas no 2, a heavy type

Opening day of the Alford & Sutton Tramway at Alford, 2nd April 1884. Locomotive no 2, used for the occasion, came from London's Merryweather & Sons, well known for its fire engines. The tramway lasted only 5$^{1}/_{2}$ years. (Picture: Alford Manor House Museum collection)

locomotive built in 1884 of around eight tons and with a horizontal boiler, came from London's Merryweather & Sons, famous for its fire engines. No 3 with its locomotive type boiler, acquired in 1885, was built at Kilmarnock by Dick, Kerr & Co which had meantime taken over W B Dick & Co, the tramway's builders. The number of passenger cars and wagons possessed is not known but records suggest there were four single-deck 4-wheeled cars and one single-deck 8-wheeled car. It is believed that the latter was the one photographed at Alford on opening day.

During its life the tramway was popular with the local residents but travel was not cheap. The adult return fare was one shilling (5p) and half price for children. Parcels, newspapers and luggage were also carried and goods traffic flourished. The locomotives and cars were maintained in excellent condition and men would daily walk the line to clear the rails of stones or anything that might cause damage. Unhappily, however, this state of affairs was not allowed to continue for in 1884 work began on a new railway from Willoughby to Sutton, thus spelling financial ruin to the tramway.

The railway opened two years later on 14th October 1886 and, two years later, on 14th July 1888 the line extended to Mablethorpe. The line crossed the tramway just outside Sutton and this was how Tramway Crossing signal box, built and manned by the GNR, acquired its name. Tramway receipts began to fall to the extent that closure seemed inevitable. A regular service was maintained for a time but in November 1889 the tramway company's manager left for a better position. By early December the trams stopped running. The *Lincoln Gazette* of 7th December 1889 reported, 'The Alford & Sutton Tramway has ceased to run its cars, ostensibly for the winter months, but really for an indefinite period. This stoppage will prove a great loss to the tradesmen of Alford as many people travelled by tram to the town to make their purchases'. The tradesmen and many well-to-do folk of Alford were given the chance to purchase the tramway for a mere £500 but when they responded with an offer of £300 it was, needless to say, turned down. In consequence the tramway closed for good and a year or so later the rails were removed.

At Alford the tramway sheds were demolished as recently as 1989 but the office is still there – still known as Argyle House. It is today a private residence owned by the proprietor of Hunts Coaches which has been established at the site for over 60 years. At Sutton-on-Sea the sheds have gone with their place now occupied by private residences known as Alford Court. To the author when visiting the area, it seemed really surprising that accounts of this short-lived tramway of less than six years which closed over a century ago should still be remembered by quite a number of people.

Chapter 10

TRAMS IN A CATHEDRAL CITY

(The Peterborough Electric Traction Co)

'Peterborough's electric trams are no more! Their death has been long and lingering, but none the less slow but sure, to the great relief of all concerned. They have retired creaking and groaning with age, a few at a time; the funeral has been drawn out, until at last the hardiest car of the bunch has got so tired of wandering to Walton, nosing to Newark and dashing down to Dogsthorpe that it has thought fit to go to the retired list'. So wrote a reporter of the *Peterborough Citizen* in its edition of 18th November 1930 following the closure of the city's tramway system three days earlier.

Twenty seven years earlier the mood had been quite different. When the first car left the Market Place at noon on Saturday, 24th January 1903, the crowds were so dense that many were left behind. The *Peterborough Citizen* reported that by 3 pm the car had carried 600 passengers-200 an hour! Other cars soon followed equally packed with passengers. Yet the day was not without its humorous incidents. In the publication *Peterborough Tramways*, G D Austin writes that an elderly lady from the country was so lost in admiration of the trams that she let her purse drop to the ground instead of into her pocket. Fortunately for her it was found by Mrs Barlow, wife of the Dean of Peterborough who handed it to the police who later returned it to the worried passenger.

Car no 3 in Long Causeway looking towards Barrett's Corner c1910. Peterborough's tramway system was a small one comprising in all 14 cars and a track-watering vehicle. All came from the Brush Electrical Engineering works at Loughborough. (Lens of Sutton)

Perhaps more bizarre was the consternation caused when a labourer on Market Hill saw a tramcar approaching Long Causeway from Westgate Corner and thought it was a Great Northern Railway train which had broken loose and such was his fear that he immediately had a fit. The incident caused quite an upset among the onlookers and it took seven or eight men to hold down the terrified man. That evening a minor incident had a happier ending. A domestic cat crossing Lincoln Road crouched with fear as a tram approached with its blaze of light – right in the car's path. The driver humanely stopped the tram thinking he had run the cat over but on checking found the animal in the lifeguard at the front and all was well. Despite the saving of its life, the cat greatly resented all efforts to dislodge it.

Henry VIII gave Peterborough on the river Nene its cathedral status in 1541 and its town hall was built in 1671. Before the railways came, Peterborough was a compact market town clustered around its cathedral but when the Great Northern Railway built locomotive sheds at New England in 1853, a ribbon development of houses soon linked the two areas. During the years 1879/1880 efforts were made to build a horse tramway but none succeeded. This was despite the granting of a Provisional Order in 1880 under the 1870 Tramway Act to build a line from Crown Street (near the locomotive depot) to Peterborough North station (along Cowgate) with routes through the city centre via New Road and via Westgate.

Peterborough's electric tramway system was a comparatively small one with, at most, 14 cars and a track-watering car which could also be used as a snow-plough. Powers had been sought in 1899 by the British Electric Traction Co Ltd (BET) for lines to Walton, Dogsthorpe, Newark, Woodston and Stanground. A line to Stanground and a circular route through Woodston were refused because Narrow Bridge Street was, as its name implies, too narrow and also because of the difficulties in crossing the Great Eastern Railway line on the same level. Work to construct the remaining routes began on 12th May 1902 but even this was not without its difficulties.

Long Causeway c1906. Car no 11 awaits return to the Lincoln Road depot. The city's trams operated on a 3 ft 6 in gauge track with current collection from overhead wires. (Lens of Sutton)

A Walton-bound car no 9 in Westgate with Midgate beyond. During the tramway system's life trams carried some 50 million passengers and covered between 6 and 7 million miles. (Lens of Sutton)

One instance during October 1902 came about when the contractors were asked by the council to stop work for a week because of traffic congestion during Bridge Fair. The contractors refused so the council surveyor impounded the tar boilers and equipment locking them up in the council depot yard. The contractors obtained further supplies and hired a number of hefty Irish labourers to stand guard over the work. There were complaints too about the labourers and a councillor claimed the workers were rough and uncouth. 'It is shameful', he said, 'that young ladies of genteel upbringing cannot go out for a walk without having to avert their gaze and block up their ears'.

The 3 ft 6 in gauge overhead wire system opened on 24th January 1903 between Walton and Long Causeway with a route to Dogsthorpe following one week later. Newark was reached on 28th March 1903 giving a total route length of just over 5 miles. A depot and offices were built in Lincoln Road at a cost of £3,000. The depot consisted of five roads which converged to a single line junction in Lincoln Road facing the city. The points were unusual since they were changed by railway-type point levers.

The cars, all open-topped and supplied by the Brush Electrical Engineering Co Ltd at Loughborough, were each equipped with two motors, each of 17 hp sufficient for the town's level terrain. The first 12 cars seated 22 passengers inside and 26 outside (on top) on transverse reversible wooden garden-type seats. The original order had been for 14 cars but the last two went instead to the South Staffordshire Tramways to become nos 28 and 29. Cars 14 and 15 (no number 13!) acquired two years later accommodated 28 on top. These were intended originally for Worcester but were diverted to Peterborough. The livery was lake brown and cream except for the Worcester cars which remained the holly green and cream of the Worcester company until repainted.

80

In 1907 the turbine manufacturing company, Peter Brotherhood, came to Peterborough from London which meant increased passengers on the Walton route. This lead eventually to three extra trams being allocated to the early morning workmen's service. These were usually packed to capacity even to the point that overflow passengers had to hang to the outside of the car. The Peter Brotherhood company was sited just north of the Midland & Great Northern Railway (M&GN) bridge across Lincoln Road. This acquired the name of Rhubarb Bridge when the line was built in 1866 since the embankments had been built up from nearby farms and rhubarb roots continued to flourish in the soil for many years.

During the First World War women and temporary drivers were recruited, as in other systems, to take the place of those called to the front. Headlamps were masked as a precaution against Zeppelin raids. In the event of a raid drivers were instructed to put out all lights and return to the depot immediately. Spares became difficult to obtain with manufacturers engaged on war work and services were curtailed, particularly on the Newark and Dogsthorpe routes. During 1916 Peterborough had not only the war to contend with but also weather of a violence hitherto unknown. A thunderstorm which started early in the morning on 28th March continued until 6 pm that evening when it was followed by a hurricane and a very heavy fall of snow. There was considerable damage with many telegraph poles blown down, some at Walton falling across the tramway's overhead wires halting services. The town was practically cut off and trams were disrupted for some considerable time.

During the General Strike in 1926 the trams stopped completely. A temporary bus service was organised manned by volunteers although the *Peterborough Citizen* was careful not to give names in its report but merely called them 'distinguished young citizens' and the conductresses 'dainty young misses of good family'. Yet the buses were no newcomers to the city's streets since the tramway company had been running bus services to areas not covered by

Westgate and Midgate, Peterborough, viewed in September 1990. There is virtually nothing left of the old tramway – the Lincoln Road depot now serves buses with the original tram shed partly rebuilt and the track removed. (Author)

trams since as early as 1913. In 1930 the company approached the city council to obtain its views on abandoning the trams altogether. A sub-committee was established and it was provisionally agreed the trams should operate for the greater part of 1930 with abandonment commencing on Monday, 4th August of that year.

This arrangement began as agreed with double-decker buses operating various routes. Yet since official authority to abandon the trams had not yet been given, the company was obliged to continue its services to maintain statutory rights. This was carried out by running a single car over each route from 6 am to 7 pm, a vehicle that was quickly named by the local press as 'the ghost tram'. Eventually on Saturday, 15th November 1930, at 2.40 pm the 'ghost tram' began its last journey from the Market Place to the depot. The driver was motorman E J Jennings who had driven the first service car on 24th January 1903 and the conductress was Miss G Coles. There were ten passengers.

Thus ended 27 years of faithful service with the trams having travelled between 6 and 7 million miles and having carried some 50

Car no 11 at Long Causeway c1906. Trams were proposed to the south side of Peterborough but lines were never built because of narrow streets and also because the Great Eastern Railway strongly objected to a crossing over their tracks. (Lens of Sutton)

Long Causeway from Cathedral Square photographed in September 1990. The trams went over 60 years ago and today the area is pedestrianised. (Author)

million passengers. Today there is very little to show that the trams existed. Several car bodies went to serve on farms and in 1975 one still existed in Crown Street, Peterborough, in use as a green house. By the early 1970s all traces of tram standards had gone. The depot in Lincoln Road became a bus depot with the original tram building truncated and the track removed. A member of the staff at the depot proudly claimed he had a yard length of tram track at his home!

After closure of the tram services the *Peterborough Advertiser* announced in heavy type, 'The Trams have all gone to the Big Tram Depot in the Sky'. The *Peterborough Citizen* wrote less dramatically, 'Our famous trams are no more. They came, heralded by the whole populace. They went unhonoured and unsung'.

Chapter 11

TRAMS SERVE THE SHOE INDUSTRY

(Northampton Street Tramways Company and Northampton
Corporation Tramways)

Northampton Street Tramways Company

Northampton saw its first public tramway system at 6 pm on 4th
June 1881. Four cars hauled by horses decorated with rosettes and
ribbons were put into service from Kingsley Road along Kettering
Road to the western end of Abington Street. The cars were
'crowded to excess, and great commotion was caused along the
route, hearty cheers being given by large crowds as the different
cars passed to and fro'. The Board of Trade inspection had taken
place only that morning and a ceremonial first journey had taken
place at noon followed by a luncheon at the Plough Hotel where
many speeches were made.

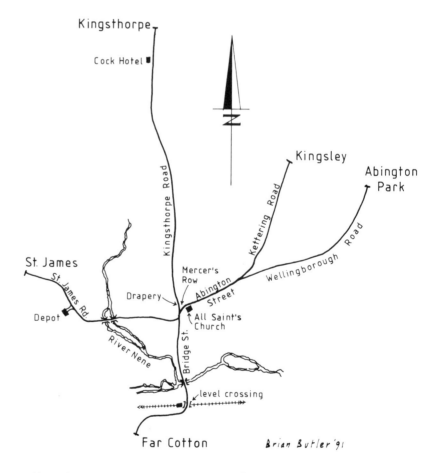

Northampton Corporation Tramways

Northampton is a town with a long and eventful history. It is reputed to be the final resting place of Boadicea but no-one is quite sure of the exact site. It has been said that Whittlebury Forest holds the secret. On the London Road the Eleanor Cross is one of the few survivors of the crosses which marked Queen Eleanor's funeral procession from Harby (Nottingham) to Westminster Abbey in 1290. It was placed there by a grieving King Edward I to mark where his wife's funeral cortege rested on its journey. In 1675 the whole of the town's centre (600 houses) was gutted by fire. In 1870 the town with its thriving cattle markets had a population of 45,000 but this increased dramatically to around 60,000 by 1880 as the shoe and associated leather trade became the staple trade of the area.

At that time, many other industrial towns had gone over to the factory system but, in Northampton, a lot of the leather work was carried out in workers' own homes spread across the area. In

Tracklaying in Kettering Road in 1904 – the first route to convert from horse trams to electric. (Picture: courtesy John Horrocks, Director of Engineering & Supplies, Northampton Transport Ltd)

consequence, a transport system became necessary. On 9th January 1880 a meeting was held in London at which the Northampton Street Tramways Company was formed. Later that year Parliament gave the go-ahead for a horse tramway to be built and in March 1881 work began on a 3 ft 6 in gauge system in Kettering Road. Stables and a small car shed were built on land behind 72, Abington Street and six cars were ordered from the Birmingham Carriage & Wagon Company at Smethwick. Four arrived in time for the opening being small six window double-deck cars, accommodating 18 inside with 18 outside on knife-boards seats.

Further lines were soon to follow. On 7th October 1881 horse trams commenced services from the Drapery to St George's Terrace, Kingsthorpe Road, and two further cars arrived in an endeavour to meet demand. Yet it seemed there were still not enough, for protests were made about overcrowding of cars and the overworking of horses. The RSPCA became involved but no case was ever proven against the company. Lines further extended and by 1883 Kingsthorpe village was reached. This was a journey of just under two miles with a tram taking around 25 minutes, yet it was claimed by the sturdy it could be walked in almost the same time!

At this stage there were two interesting innovations. In the 1975 Spring and Summer editions of *Tramway Review*, A W Brotchie wrote that had capital been available then steam power would have been attempted. As it was, a gas powered locomotive was tried having been built locally at Mobb's Vulcan Ironworks in Guildhall Road. Experiments were mostly confined to the depot but on 3rd March 1883 it did successfully haul a car near West Bridge containing a dozen people. It was said modifications were needed

Passengers and onlookers celebrate the opening of the electric tramway service on 21st July 1904 at the Abington Park terminus. (Lens of Sutton)

The Drapery, not long after Northampton's electric trams began in 1904. At most the system had 37 cars and the livery was red and white with black and gold lining around the panels. (Lens of Sutton)

but nothing further was heard. It was claimed this may well have been the first occasion ever using the internal combustion engine for road transport. A second experiment was taken a little less seriously. The proprietor of a local cycle works built a two-geared treadle cycle to pull trams. Only sparse details are available but it is thought it had four driving wheels each about 4 ft in diameter and possibly flanged. One gear was for 'power' and the other for 'speed'. The idea was soon forgotten.

During 1886 the company's finances became strained so three double-deck cars were converted to single-deck one-horse cars. These proved successful so four were purchased, also from the Birmingham carriage works, at a cost of £105 each. At its most the town's horse tram fleet numbered 22 cars. In 1892 Mansfield opened a boot factory and a tramway extension along Wellingborough Road to Roseholme Road opened on 18th May 1893. The following year a car was fitted experimentally with electric lights powered from accumulators but the idea did not last.

On 21st October 1901 the tramway company was taken over by

The Drapery, photographed in September 1990. A few buildings remained relatively unaltered but the trams went nearly 60 years ago. (Author)

Car no 16 bound for Kingsley Park photographed outside the North Western Hotel c1910 in Northampton's Mare Fair. The town's trams lasted until December 1934. (Lens of Sutton)

the corporation. Earlier that year, on 20th April, there had been a serious accident when car no 15 overturned causing many injuries and one subsequent death. Complaints had already been made about inadequate brakes but on the day in question, a Saturday, the car was making its way down Abington Street to a football match with a full load aboard when the brakes failed completely. The car gathered speed with the horses galloping faster and faster and at the corner of Wood Hill it overturned. Twenty people were injured, many hurt by jumping off the car prematurely. Despite the accident, the car suffered little damage and only four windows were broken.

The corporation soon set about improving the services but efforts were ultimately directed towards scrapping the horse trams and providing an electric service. Work to reconstruct the lines began in January 1904 but this was held up for a time when labourers unsuccessfully went on strike to secure an increase from 5½d (just over 2p) to 6d (2½p) per hour. It was reckoned that the horse trams had run over 2 million miles and carried 28 million passengers.

Northampton Corporation Tramways
The town's electric tramway system began at 3.30 pm on 21st July 1904 when four decorated cars toured the routes to finish at Abington Park where guests had a special tea followed by speeches. The gauge had been retained at 3 ft 6 ins and current collection was from overhead wires. The contractor had been J G White & Co of London at a cost of £85,000 for the initial five mile system. The first lines to be completed were from St James to Kettering Road and Wellingborough Road. On 19th August 1904 electric trams took over the Kingsthorpe route and the horse trams were sold off, the latter realising between £4 and £7 each. A number of horses were retained for the Far Cotton bus, an area that had so far remained without a tramway service.

Business was brisk from the beginning. In *Tramway Review,*

88

Winter 1986 edition, D R Howard wrote that when public services began on 4.30 pm on 21st July some 11,644 passengers were carried within the first six hours. Two days later, on the Saturday, 27,000 people used the trams. On the Sunday there was a complaint from All Saints where it was claimed that the noise of the trams interrupted the sermon and on Monday a milk float driver misjudged a tram's speed and a collision resulted. Despite these minor incidents the trams proved immediately popular.

The central tram terminus was by All Saints church using the double tracks in the immediately adjacent streets of Mercers Row and Drapery. Trams reached St James to the west, passing the depot in St James Road and terminating at St James End near Franklins Gardens in Weedon Road. To the north trams reached Cranford Road at Kingsthorpe and eastwards, services reached Kingsley terminating at St Matthews church and Abington Park by the park gates.

Northampton's first 20 cars came from the Dick, Kerr & Co Ltd at Preston. These were standard three side window and open top

Buses today have replaced the trams at Kingsthorpe. When the town's trams began in 1904 they were immediately popular with over 11,000 passengers carried in the first six hours! (Author)

89

One of the four single-deck bogie cars supplied by the English Electric Co in 1922 seen here at Franklins Gardens awaiting return to All Saints. The cars acquired the nickname of 'tanks'. (Colin Withey collection)

Car no 19 outside Northampton's Westminster Bank in the late 1920s. This was one of 20 cars supplied by the Dick, Kerr works at Preston in 1904 for the start of the system. The top cover was added in 1926. (Colin Withey collection)

models seating 22 inside on longitudinal veneer seats plus 24 on top on wooden transverse seats. The cars were mounted on Brill trucks and each had two 27 hp motors. Since the majority of the trams were in use daily, two further cars were ordered from Dick, Kerr in March 1905.

There was a special event in September 1907 when the longest serving tramcar driver, Jack Adams at the age of 55, married Miss M Higgins at All Saints church. After the ceremony the couple and their guests travelled in a specially decorated car to a reception at Franklins Gardens, attended also by other tramway department employees. It is believed this was the only occasion in North-ampton that a tram was used for such a purpose.

In 1911 an Act was passed allowing the corporation to build a

number of extensions. These included a line along the north side of Abington Park, a link between the Cock Hotel at Kingsthorpe and the Abington Park terminus, an extension beyond St James to the Red Rover public house and, probably the most important, from the Drapery to Far Cotton. In addition to the above, trackless trolley vehicles (trolleybuses) were agreed to run from the Drapery along Billing Road to the borough boundary. No immediate action was taken on any of these issues, during which time the residents of Far Cotton had to remain content with their horse bus service.

In early 1914, the problems anticipated in running trams on the steep gradient down Bridge Street, crossing the river Nene, as well as negotiating the London Road level crossing, were finally resolved and this allowed the construction of a tram route to Far Cotton to go ahead. Semaphore signals were installed at the level crossing, controlled by the railway signal box, to safeguard the passage of trams across the railway track. Trams finally reached Far Cotton on 23rd October 1914 and, to meet demand, six further cars were ordered from the Brush Electrical Engineering Co of Loughborough. These were again four-wheel double-deck trams but, new to the town, they had covered tops and drivers' windscreens. Meantime the country had become heavily involved with the First World War and no decisions were made on the other 1911 proposals.

On 28th March 1916 Northampton suffered a terrible blizzard equal in severity to that at Peterborough (see chapter 10) and trams came to a virtual standstill as drivers and conductors tried to dig their way through. When the thaw came there were serious floods at St James and on the Far Cotton route. The war of course made its impact on the system with lights dimmed as a precaution against

A tram shelter which has survived the years at Kingsthorpe opposite the Cock Inn. Recently renovated, there are hopes it might become a listed building. (Author)

Northampton's tramcar no 21 has survived the years, currently under restoration at Tal-y-Cafn in North Wales by the Llandudno & Colwyn Bay Electric Railway Society. On the platform, David Smith, chairman of the Society. (Picture: courtesy Llandudno & Colwyn Bay Electric Railway Society)

air raids and, as elsewhere, conductresses replacing men who had gone to the front.

Early in 1922 the last additions were made to the fleet when four single-deck saloon bogie cars were supplied by the English Electric Co Ltd. Each could seat 42 passengers and there were ten sash windows each side which could be opened, although protected by rails outside to stop people leaning out. The cars were 40 ft long overall and at the top of Bridge Street it was necessary to put a notice reading 'Beware Tram Swinging Out'. With doors at both ends for passenger flow, these cars took great loads and acquired the nickname of 'tanks'.

Despite the earlier 1911 proposal, trolleybuses never came to Northampton and instead, in 1922, motorbuses were tried from the town centre along Billing Road and Abington Park as well as reaching St James and the Cock Hotel at Kingsthorpe. With the vehicles running on solid tyres, they could hardly have been comfortable. Meanwhile much of the original track had deteriorated badly and, with occasional repairs in hand, services became delayed. Such was the decline of the tramway system that in 1926 consideration was given to replacing the trams to Far Cotton with motor buses but it was considered such a move was 'premature'.

In September 1928, two new 'Guy' six-wheel double-deck buses were introduced along the Wellingborough Road route where the tram track was considered beyond economic repair. For a time a mixed service operated but when the buses proved successful, the tramcar service to Abington Park was abandoned. This took place on 20th April 1929. With buses proving successful, the possibility of relaying track along the Kingsley route was now decided against and regular buses were introduced. When trams stopped running to Kingsley on 31st August 1930, complete closure of the system was in sight.

The end for Kingsthorpe's trams came on 26th September 1933. A proposal to replace them with trolleybuses had been turned down and motor buses were introduced. Only two routes now remained, these being to St James and to Far Cotton. On the latter, sections of track had been recently relaid yet, despite this, the end was not far off. The final closure came eventually on 15th December 1934 when car no 29 was driven by Alderman A L Chown, Chairman of the Transport Committee, with the Borough Treasurer as conductor. According to the *Chronicle and Echo*, the tram was driven from All Saints to the depot 'rather erratically'. Thirty years of electric trams in Northampton had come to an end.

Happily in 1990, the author found when visiting the town there were numerous relics to recall those early times. Large pictures showing trams in the 1920s were found on the walls at the Tesco Superstore in Mereway and also at the local rates office in the town centre. Opposite the Cock Inn at Kingsthorpe a fine-looking tram shelter had survived the years. Recently renovated – and sadly vandalised again – there was a possibility it may become a listed monument. The 1904-built tram depot in St James Road is today a bus depot yet some trackwork and a point could still be seen inside the building. Also at the depot there was a hand cart which formerly belonged to the Tramway Parcels department.

When the trams ceased, most were sold as scrap and some were used locally as sheds. Fortunately the body of one has survived – car no 21 supplied by Dick, Kerr in 1905. This is currently in the hands of the Llandudno & Colwyn Bay Electric Railway Society, a former tramway that also used the same 3 ft 6 ins gauge. A great deal of restoration work has already been carried out with posts replaced where rot has been found, new waist and rocker panels fitted, new ventilator window frames made and fitted, and so on. Also a complete new stairway has been made to replace stairs missing from one end, although these are not yet fitted.

Completion of Northampton 21 depends partly on the society obtaining a 21E truck and partly on having a building high enough to fit top deck railings and trolley. When finished it is hoped it can be displayed in the Llandudno area – what a proud moment it will be for those responsible after so many years of such splendid restoration work.

Chapter 12

HORSE TRAMS IN A UNIVERSITY CITY

(Cambridge Street Tramways Co)

Passers-by in the streets of Cambridge would have been surprised one day in the early 1880s to see two men pulling a tramcar carrying 57 passengers, from the railway station to the post office. The car made five stops along the route – and the men did not suffer any great strain. The action was taken by the Cambridge Street Tramway Company which, frustrated by continual accusations that its horses were ill-treated, decided to stage the experiment. Yet it was to no avail and sections of the public remained unconvinced.

In August 1851, Cambridge's first horse-buses appeared. They were double-deckers, each drawn by four horses providing a service between Cambridge and Shepreth to connect with trains from London's Kings Cross. When the line from Shepreth was extended to Cambridge in 1852, the buses were withdrawn. In 1878 plans for horse-drawn trams were announced and two companies, each called Cambridge Tramways Company, submitted schemes. The first company proposed routes across the city centre to a gauge of 3 ft 6 ins but the other was less ambitious. It put forward ideas for a 4 ft 8½ in system from the station to the city centre plus another from Hyde Park Corner along Trumpington Street to serve the universities.

The second company was adopted but, bearing in mind the city's narrow streets, a narrower gauge was required. In 1879 the Cambridge Street Tramway Company (CST) was formed and a

An early picture of Cambridge single-deck car no 2 between the post office and the station, c1880s. The poor state of the road is much in evidence. (Cambridgeshire Collection)

3 ft 6 in gauge was proposed but this changed to 4 ft before construction began. A Bill received Royal Assent on 21st July 1879 and work quickly went ahead. In his book, *Cambridge Street Tramways*, S L Swingle wrote that on 13th October 1880 a single-deck car was tried out, but there was difficulty in negotiating the section by Great St Mary's church because the gauge of the temporarily laid rails was incorrect. A further trial two days later proved successful.

The first section of the tramway opened officially on 28th October 1880 carrying passengers from the railway station along St Andrew's Street to the post office opposite Christ's College. Six cars were used and on the next day it was recorded that 801 people used the trams. The cars, comprising two double-deck open-top and four single-deck vehicles, were built by the Starbuck Car &

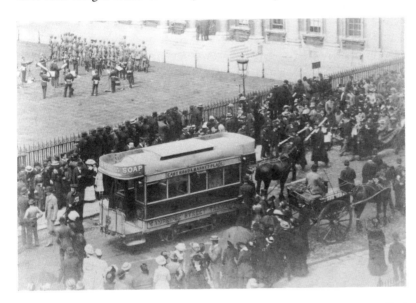

Horse tram no 5, c1890, outside the Senate House amid a University procession. Only single-deck cars were used on the Trumpington Road route. (Cambridgeshire Collection)

Cambridge's double-deck horse-tram no 7 waits at the Post Office terminus in 1904 before returning to the railway station. (Cambridgeshire Collection)

Wagon Company. They cost £300 each and were designed for one-horse working and the livery was red and cream. There was difficulty initially in finding a suitable place to house the trams and horses and they were accommodated for a time in the goods yard at the railway station. Later, in January 1881, the depot and stables were moved to 184, East Road, where the CST's registered office was situated.

The Cambridge Street Tramways (Extension) Order of 1880 agreed further routes. In November 1880 a line from Hyde Park Corner via Lensfield Road and Trumpington Road opened to Market Hill and, later the same month, trams were reaching East Road via Gonville Place. At the same time, further sections of tramway were authorised but these never materialised and the route mileage remained at 2.69 miles. Had one been completed, trams would have extended further along East Road into Newmarket Road. This line never went beyond the junction of Fitzroy Street, just beyond the January 1881 depot. Another line, opposed by the Masters and Fellows of Emmanuel College, would have provided a circular route round part of the city. From East Road, trams would have passed along Maids' Causeway to enter Emmanuel Road and Emmanuel Street to join the existing line in St Andrew's Street.

Public complaints about the over-working of horses continued. Letters appeared in the *Cambridge Chronicle* and *Independent Press* stating that the horses were suffering because of heavy loads. It was pointed out that the need to continually stop and start a car carrying forty or more passengers put such a strain on a single horse that two should be used per tram. The idea was tried for a time but it did not last since there were no gradients of note anywhere in the system.

Despite a fleet of only six cars, a pretty frequent service was maintained. Throughout the day, trams ran every ten minutes from the station to the post office and every seven minutes at busier times. Fares on any route were 2d (less than 1p) all the way or 1d (less than ½p) from Hyde Park Corner. Season tickets could be purchased at 6s (30p) a month or up to £2.10s. for a year. Small animals or poultry could be carried at ½d per head but this was rarely put into practice.

The trams were used by many passengers to connect with trains, so it was important that time should not be lost. Yet this was not the case, for 'up' cars to the station frequently had to wait along the route to pass 'down' cars since much of the track was single and loops had not been provided. It was not until 1885 that a passing place was constructed in Station Road. Yet the company flourished, more horses were purchased and the permanent way was improved. There were complaints that the trams were noisy and considerable money was spent to fit new wheels and noiseless springs.

There was a dispute in 1890 between the CST and the council over roadway maintenance. The 1879 Act carried a clause requiring the tramway company to repair 'the highways in which the rails were laid'. This caused much concern but the matter was resolved in 1892 when the council agreed to take over the liability, provided the tramway company paid an annual sum of £325 by quarterly instalments over a period of 25 years. Under the arrangement, the CST undertook to keep the sleepers, rails and concrete bed in good order while the council maintained the road.

During 1894 another double-deck tramcar (no 7) was purchased from Starbuck. This, like earlier double-deckers, could seat 18 in the saloon but 23 (one extra) on top. In the same year, the company's profits benefited when Cambridge held a Royal Show,

Horse trams and motor buses in competition, 1912. The Ortona Motor Company commenced services in 1907 and it was not long before they successfully operated over tramway routes. The trams lasted until February 1914. (Cambridgeshire Collection)

The remains of a Cambridge tram body photographed c1960 in a garden at Haddenham in use as a tool shed. Sadly the tram body no longer exists today. (Picture: Maurice Kidd)

with trams carrying many additional passengers during the event. In May 1895 there was a plan for trams to reach the village of Newnham from Trumpington Road by a proposed viaduct road across the meadows. According to the *Cambridge Chronicle*, this would allow 'the people from the slums and alleys of our congested, unhealthy towns into the green lanes and fair meadow land.' Alas, the scheme did not succeed.

A setback to the fortunes of the CST came in 1896 when the Cambridge Omnibus Company was granted a licence to operate eight two-horse buses in the town and suburbs. This incensed the CST since the buses planned to operate a standard 1d fare from the station to the town (the trams were still 2d) and also since the CST were paying £325 a year for road repairs while the buses used the roads free of charge. The public were in favour of the buses, so the CST countered the challenge by purchasing four single-deck buses and introducing its own standard 1d fare. The buses were specially made for the CST and, because of their rather unusual design, they acquired the nickname of 'bathing machines'.

The CST suffered badly against the competition and in the end it was the omnibus company that offered a solution. In 1900 it agreed to withdraw its buses from tram routes if the CST withdrew its buses from the rest of the city. The CST sold its buses to its ex-competitor and tramway receipts improved. The bus company was less fortunate, lasting only until 1902 when it went out of business.

Meantime in 1898 the British Electric Traction Co Ltd purchased shares in the CST and proposed an electric tramway system. At about the same time the council applied for powers to municipalise the CST also with a view to electrification. No agreement was reached and in 1904 the BET sold its shares to the Cambridge Electric Traction Syndicate, a subsidiary of the city's electric supply company, which was also interested in electric trams. A public meeting was held to debate the possibility but the idea was opposed because of costs and also objections to overhead power lines.

In 1905 ideas of electric trams were shelved when two motor bus companies commenced services. Known as the 'Cambridge Light Blue Co' and the 'Cambridge Motor Bus Co', rivalry between the concerns was strong. The 'Light Blues' lasted only six months and the second company lost its licence in September 1906. For almost a year the trams held their own but, in August 1907, the old Cambridge Motor Bus Co was bought up and re-launched as the Ortona Motor Co, with its fleet of green buses. Offices were at 112, Hills Road (later the depot of the Eastern Counties Omnibus Co), and it was not long before double-deck buses were successfully operating over tramway routes.

In 1909 a further car, a double-deck open-top, was purchased for £160 (making eight in all). Yet CST revenue continued to suffer, worsened by the £325 a year payable for road upkeep. By 1912 the CST was in arrears and in September 1913, a writ was issued against the CST for amounts outstanding. In January 1914, a petition was filed for the compulsory winding-up of the company. The motor buses had won the day – partly at the expense of the tramway company.

The end for the horse trams came on Wednesday, 18th February 1914. Local residents enjoyed last rides on the cars that had served them for 34 years and children were encouraged to travel so they might remember the trams in future years. A mock funeral service was held by undergraduates, many wearing surplices and chanting a dirge. The official last car left the railway station at 6.25 pm driven by Ephraim Skinner, the company's oldest driver. Two days later, at an auction attended by around 600 people, sales included the cars themselves which fetched between £7 15s (£7.75) and £15 each.

Today the former tram depot at East Street has been redeveloped although some of the original buildings have been converted to offices. There is another reminder of the old days at the Cambridge Museum of Technology in Cheddars Lane, where a section of tram track has been preserved and is on display. There is also a reversible type wooden seat but the slats forming the seat and back are modern replacements.

The following was part of a poem written by a driver to his horse after the closure of the tramway:

> What will I do when you are gone?
> All day in sun and rain,
> From Station to the Post Office
> I'll walk and back again.
> But oh! An awful thought occurs,
> That fills me with dismay.
> They're sure to pull the tramlines up
> And I shan't know my way.

Chapter 13

A TRAMWAY SYSTEM IN BEDFORDSHIRE

(Luton Corporation Tramways)

There was considerable embarrassment when Luton's tramway system was officially opened on 21st February 1908. The council had assumed that Mr Lloyd George, President of the Board of Trade, would perform the ceremony but it transpired his diary was full. Other dignitaries were contacted but in view of the short notice many must have been aware they were not first choice. Important people such as the Duke of Bedford and the Mayors of Bedford and St Albans all turned it down while others claimed they were 'unwell'. Eventually the local Liberal MP, Mr T Gair-Ashton, accepted, no doubt conscious he might lose votes if he declined.

There were three routes and the total length of track was a mere 6½ miles. The system never expanded and the initial fleet comprised 12 tramcars. On the opening day, cars 1, 2 and 3 were decorated with red, white and blue bunting and they travelled all the routes to end at the Town Hall where a civic luncheon was held. According to records it was a bitterly cold day and Mr Gair-Ashton, the Liberal MP, really did have a bad cold. Nevertheless the system proved successful and, according to *The Luton Times*, many were fascinated by the sight of 'illuminated electric tramcars gliding along the street'.

First thoughts of electric trams in Luton came after the Borough Council had completed a power station in 1898. Bristol had been

Luton's tramway system was officially opened on 21st February 1908 and trams were suitably decorated for the occasion. (Colin Withey collection)

operating electric trams since 1895 and Dover in Kent had followed two years later. An Electricity and Tramways Committee was established and in 1905 Parliament agreed that the council could go ahead. The firm of J G White and Co was appointed to undertake the work.

Construction began in October 1907 and the work was finished in less than five months, despite bad weather, at a total cost of £63,000. Originally a gauge of 3 ft 6 ins had been proposed but for safety reasons the standard 4 ft 8½ ins gauge was adopted. This was in spite of various objections from a number of factories and shops, including Boots the Chemists, who claimed it would reduce the roadside loading space for their horse drawn wagons.

Efforts were made to keep the dates of trial runs secret but when trams turned out after midnight there were large crowds looking on. In one instance a car jammed on a curve and the passengers had to get out and push it a few yards until it was free. The trials proved highly successful and the Board of Trade gave the go-ahead on 18th February, three days before the official opening. A maximum speed limit of 12 mph was established reducing to 4 mph on all curves and points and a number of downhill runs.

The three routes ran from the Park Street depot to Round Green, from Park Square to the end of Kingsway and from the London Road, opposite the end of Tennyson Road, to Wardown. All routes passed through George Street which meant a strict timetable was necessary. In addition the system was single track with only a few passing loops so that trams could pass each other. A number of steep hills existed, particularly Midland Road, yet brake failures occurred on only a few occasions.

The twelve cars were all double-deckers with open tops. Each seated 22 inside on longitudinal wooden seats and 32 on top on transverse garden type wooden seats with reversible backs. At a terminus a conductor would shout 'All Change' and then walk the upper deck crashing the seat backs to face the reverse direction.

Car no 12 in Luton's Park Street soon after the system opened in 1908. Drivers were exposed to all weathers and some even claimed their cars had been struck by lightning! (Lens of Sutton)

The bodies had been built by the United Electric Car Co of Preston and painted green and cream. The words 'Luton Corporation Tramways' were written in gold letters along the side plus the Borough's Coat of Arms. Each tram had two 30 hp electric motors supplied by British Thomson-Houston.

However, the trams were hardly a total success. Many said that if you were in a hurry it could be quicker to walk. The open tops were very exposed to the elements and often in the winter the seats were coated with frost. Cyclists were critical because their wheels often got stuck in the tracks. In the early days drivers had to stand at the controls all day on eight hour shifts and for this they were paid 11½d (just under 5p) an hour. There were no windscreens and drivers were totally exposed to all weathers. According to an

Park Square, Luton

Car no 16 in Park Square. The initial fleet comprised 12 open-topped tramcars all painted green and cream with 'Luton Corporation Tramways' in gold letters along the side plus the Borough's Coat of Arms. (Lens of Sutton)

Trams pass in Luton's George Street in 1929. The town's trams survived until 1932 when they were replaced by motor buses. (Colin Withey collection)

article on Luton's Tramways published some years ago, Ivan A Jones wrote that many drivers considered that their cars had been struck by lightning in bad storms. One claimed that the electric meter situated on the bulkhead above the passenger entrance melted down an inspector's neck during such an incident at Kingsway!

Despite the strict rules endured by staff many tram drivers enjoyed their work. With only a dozen cars, they were a small group of men who came to be known by many in the town. On occasions drivers delivered parcels from one part of the town to another and often on a cold day folk would send a servant out with a cup of tea. Sometimes generous people paid a little more than necessary for their fare to help a conductor's meagre earnings or on occasions a tram would stop outside a well known citizen's house for a few extra pence to save a walk back from a stop. At Christmas there were raffles and collections towards a Tram Drivers Dinner held on more than one occasion at the Park Street depot.

In 1916 there was an accident when a tram ran out of control down Midland Road and the damage was such that it was 18 months before it was back in service. Luton later acquired another tram (no 13), a single-decker bought from Glasgow Corporation for £200. It was used mostly on the quieter Wardown route and, like many buses today, it was one man operated with the driver collecting the fares.

By the late 1920s comfortable and far less draughty motor buses were successfully competing against the trams. In an effort to improve the trams, four were fitted with roofs and enclosed top decks at a cost of £1,000. In 1932 there were efforts to increase the number of tram route miles but this did not come about. Trams were becoming an increasing problem in the narrow streets particularly where shops and hat factories had no rear entrances for

In 1930 four of Luton's open-topped trams were fitted with roofs in an effort to make them more comfortable and to compete against the growing number of buses. (Author's collection)

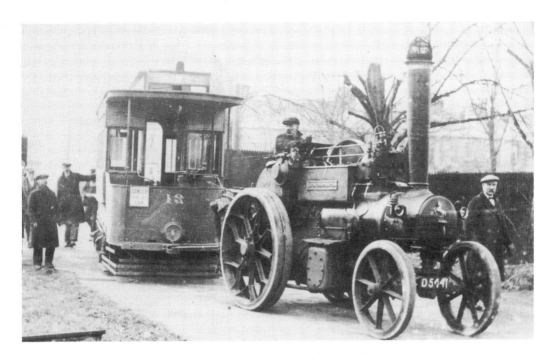

When Luton's trams closed down, this single-deck Wardown tram had to be pulled to the depot by traction engine. (Colin Withey collection)

loading and unloading. A possible solution came when the Eastern National Bus Co (later United Counties) offered the council £64,000 to phase out the trams and replace them with buses. The council accepted this by a majority vote and applied to the Ministry for acceptance.

At this point the townsfolk of Luton, many of whom had been previously critical of the trams, woke up to their possible loss and a dramatic 'Save the Trams' campaign began. After a long delay, the Ministry turned down the council's application to sell by which time the Eastern National Bus Co had lost interest. Instead the council decided to run its own buses and twelve single decker Daimlers painted dark red were purchased at a cost of £18,420.

The last tram ran in Luton on 16th April 1932. It was a sad moment for many when car no 8 came to a halt in the depot after its final run down from Round Green. Most of the drivers were retrained for the buses and within a short time tram-tracks were taken up. Meantime the trams had been towed into a yard near the depot and, according to the *Luton News*, they were sold off at £15. Many disappeared into gardens to disintegrate as the years passed but one tram is still very much in existence.

On closure of the system, car no 6 was bought for use as a site office in Dunstable to be later moved to an Oxfordshire farmyard. Thanks to the enthusiasm of Luton's museum service, it was brought back to the town so that restoration work could begin. Although in very poor condition it is hoped that at some future date it can be made fully operative again.

The tram body has no truck or stairs and the top deck has gone. The woodwork is rotten in parts but this does not deter any enthusiasm that it should be restored. When visited at the town's

105

Stockwood Craft Museum car no 6 was stored safely under wraps. Nearby stood an ex-Portuguese single-decker tram which had previously served the townspeople of Porto. It is hoped that the truck from the Portuguese tram acquired from the Black Country Museum can be adapted to suit the Luton car.

More tramway exhibits can be found at the Wardown Park Museum and Art Gallery. In addition to a 1908 Tramway Souvenir Booklet, numerous tickets as well as a reversible seat have been preserved. A splendid model can also be seen made by R L Bird of Luton and lent to the museum in 1946. When the original Park Street Depot was demolished in 1989/1990 a number of track sections were recovered and stored at Stockwood. It is thought many more sections still remain hidden beneath the tarmac of the town's roads.

If all goes well, visitors to Luton will be able to relive the past by taking a tram ride across part of Stockwood Park along over half a mile of track to reach the Stockwood Museum. Yet a great deal remains to be done. A Heritage Appeal has been launched and help from any quarter would not be refused.

Chapter 14

TRAMS AROUND A CLOCK TOWER AT LEICESTER

(Leicester Tramways Company, Leicester Corporation Tramways and Brush Electrical Engineering Co Ltd, Loughborough)

Visit the National Tramway Museum at Crich in Derbyshire and it is possible to see Leicester electric tramcar no 76. With such ornate ceilings in the saloons and beautifully carved interior wood-work, the tram does credit to the museum members who worked so hard to restore it to its present condition. Originally built as an open-top car, Leicester no 76 was top covered in 1921 or 1922. It was withdrawn from service in 1947 finding a use as a sports pavilion. It was found by museum members on a farm near Snaith in Yorkshire.

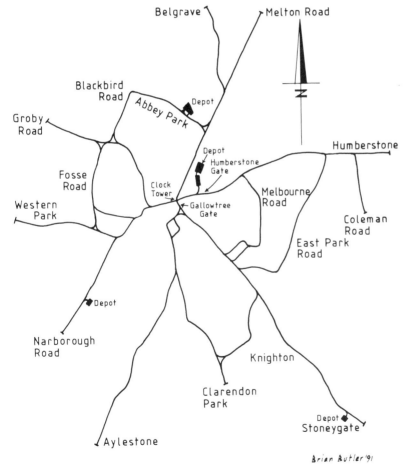

Leicester Corporation Tramways

The well known Clock Tower at Leicester. At the tramway system's peak eleven tram routes radiated outwards from this point. (Lens of Sutton)

The Clock Tower is still there but the surroundings have changed. Leicester's trams finally closed in November 1949 to give way to motor buses. (Author)

Leicester's electric tramway (1904–1949) has been described as one of the most successful of the UK's medium-sized city systems. At its most, it had 178 four-wheel double-deck cars which were fast and well maintained.

Although the majority were originally open-topped cars of rather old fashioned design, all but six were eventually covered. The town boasted eleven standard gauge routes radiating from the Clock Tower with extensions constructed even into the 1920s.

Leicester Tramways Company

Leicester's first trams were hauled by horses with a service from the Clock Tower to the Folly Inn at Belgrave beginning on Christmas Eve 1874. Standard gauge (4 ft 8½ in) rails were used and these were embedded into the carriageway to ensure that the rail surface did not protrude above road level. This had happened earlier in London causing horse-drawn carriages to have their wheels ripped off when crossing at an angle.

The three cars available came from Birkenhead where tramways

Gallowtree Gate in the town centre c1910 long before motor cars clogged the streets. (Lens of Sutton)

Gallowtree Gate in October 1990. The trams have long since gone and the street has been pedestrianised yet some of the original buildings remain. (Author)

had first begun in this country in 1860. Each car could accommodate sixteen passengers with extravagantly cushioned seating and as an added luxury there were landscape paintings on each side of the car. In the book *Leicester's Trams in Retrospect*, M S W Pearson wrote of the first trial run. Shopkeepers stood curiously in doorways and, as a car passed, crowds of small boys would follow in hot pursuit. Yet just as there was praise so was there criticism of the new service. The authorities were blamed for leaving horses in the hands of small boys with whips while the driver and conductor retired to a convenient public house. There was discontent too over the crowded cars on Sundays where it was claimed the conversation was 'unfit for the ears of decent females'.

The horse trams proved very popular and they were often full to overflowing. Extra routes were opened during 1875 and in the following year the Belgrave line saw the first steam tram tests anywhere in the country. Built at the Falcon Works at Loughborough, a machine known as the 'Hughes Patent Steam Tramway Engine' was reported as successful during trials lasting several

Cars wait at Victoria Park entrance destined for Belgrave and the Clock Tower. Electric trams came to Leicester in May 1904. (Lens of Sutton)

weeks although many noticed that 'the contraption spent more time off the rails than on them'. Despite the trials, steam trams were never used in Leicester.

As popularity continued to increase so further lines opened and certain cars were converted to double deckers with 'knife-board' seating. In 1886 the fleet reached its maximum with 46 cars bringing transport to many who could not previously afford it. Although the travellers could sit in comparative comfort, life was not easy for the staff. Many were expected to work a full seven-day week of 105 hours with a driver paid £1. 5s. a week (£1.25) and a conductor 12/6d (62½p) a week. Drivers were exposed to all weathers and were often expected to eat meals whilst on the move. They got a £1 bonus if they went a whole six months without having a horse down.

During its existence the company proved profitable. Shareholders received an annual dividend every year except during the period 1887–1890 when extensive repair work was carried out. In 1901 the corporation, well aware of changes to electric systems in many other towns, exercised its right to buy out the company with £110,210 being paid for the trams and horses plus nine miles of track. 30 horse buses were also included. Immediately discipline, previously allowed to lapse, was tightened although numerous improvements followed. Working hours were reduced, a six day week was introduced and free travel to and from work was allowed.

Meantime the council had been considering what best type of traction could be introduced. With the council initially against the idea of overhead wires, other considerations included cable haulage and a surface stud contact electric system. Less realistic proposals included propulsion by gas, internal combustion and even compressed air. These were eventually ruled out and a sub-surface conduit system was considered. When it was found this would vastly increase the costs, the council finally agreed to an overhead wire collection system.

Leicester Corporation Tramways

Work on an electric tramway system for Leicester went ahead in early 1903 causing tremendous traffic delays in the town. Streets were closed for long periods and temporary track kept horse trams going. The laying of special track at the Clock Tower, considered at the time the most complicated in the country, was however completed in record time. The layout, constructed by Hadfields of Sheffield, was finished in only ten days. The original granite sets were replaced by hardwood blocks but the complex points and cross-overs were first assembled in Hadfields' yards to ensure that they complied exactly with specification. On completion the layout was dismantled and rebuilt at the Clock Tower site. The track gauge remained the same as for the horse cars although all the rails had to be changed to cope with the extra weight of the electric cars.

The great day came on 18th May 1904. After a reception given at the Town Hall, the 300 special guests left in twelve horse trams which took them to a new power station in Painter Street. The power was ceremoniously switched on after which the party travelled by the new electric cars to the main depot in Abbey Park Road. The party transferred to three decorated trams which made a special tour of Belgrave and Stoneygate after which came more speeches and presentations at the New Walk Museum. At 7 pm public services began with all cars packed to capacity for the remainder of the day.

The bulk of the tramcars came from the Electric Railway & Tramway Carriage Works Ltd (ER&TCW), a subsidiary of the Dick, Kerr Company at Preston in Lancashire. Many would have thought the Brush Company only a few miles away at Loughborough would have been chosen. When quotations were received,

Car no 13 makes for Stoneygate along the London Road past the railway station. There was a small depot at Stoneygate but this closed to trams in 1922. (Lens of Sutton)

7615. LONDON ROAD FROM STATION.   LEICESTER.

the ER&TCW cars proved slightly more expensive but the company included a number of extras which Brush refused to add without further cost. A sample tramcar from Brush was acquired but never used and it eventually became no 191 on London's Metropolitan Electric Tramways. It was replaced by a new no 2 from Preston. Brush considered that the Dick, Kerr group had acted unfairly to gain the order and bad feeling between the two concerns existed for quite a time.

By the end of 1904 the fleet comprised 99 cars plus a water vehicle. Each car seated 22 passengers in the saloon and 34 on top. They were all open top design and four-wheeled with Brill trucks and each powered by two 25 hp motors. No bogie cars ever ran in the city. The cars were painted in deep crimson lake whereas the rocker panels, window frames and decency panels were a deep cream. In addition a single-deck water car (no 100) was acquired which could carry a load of 2,500 gallons. It could also be used for rail grinding and snow clearance.

At the start of 1906 the fleet had risen to 141 cars with the latest acquisitions having 37½ hp motors. The popularity of the system was undoubted for in the previous year over 25 million passengers were carried. Covered top cars were seen for the first time with the domed shape tops built somewhat lower than usual so they could pass under the numerous bridges. In one instance a road had to be lowered under a bridge by about two feet. The covered top cars did not prove totally satisfactory however since ventilation proved inadequate in bad weather particularly when passengers insisted on smoking. As a result of this a further batch of cars reverted to open top but were designed so that they could be converted at a later date.

Leicester's system can best be described as comprising eleven routes radiating mainly from the Clock Tower with others joining a mile or so out. In 1904 an extension beyond the Groby Road terminus had been authorised but unfortunately this was never built. Had it come about trams would have reached Anstey where

Open-topped car no 27 in London Road, c1910. Victoria Park is on the right and the junction with Evington Road on the left. (Lens of Sutton)

they would have gone on to either Groby or Newton Linford. The project had originally been put forward by Power & Traction Ltd, better known with regard to Aldershot Tramways and the Nidd Valley Railway.

An improved domed canopy with better ventilation was produced in 1912 by Dick Kerr and 19 open toppers were equipped accordingly. Just before the First World War another 20 cars were supplied. Each equipped with two 40 hp motors, these became Pay-As-You-Enter cars fitted with very large platforms where passengers could wait to pay their fares on entering the car.

During the First World War lady conductresses were employed to ease the staff shortage situation. Car 121 seen here at the depot had a Brill truck and was powered by two 35 hp motors. (Colin Withey collection)

Cars wait at the Belgrave terminus. Most of Leicester's cars were originally open-topped and the majority were covered at some stage. (Lens of Sutton)

Intending passengers were left in no doubt for large notices on the front of the car read 'PAY AS YOU ENTER CAR' and 'HAVE YOUR PENNY READY'! They were used experimentally on the Stoneygate and Narborough Road sections but discontinued after 15 months because of delays and inconvenience.

In May 1914 there was an incident which could hardly be imagined today. At that time the first car out in the morning was at 5.10 am which entailed signing on at 4.40 am. One conductor had apparently taken his dog round the block before setting out and had forgotten to replace his bowler with his uniform cap! On arrival the inspector took one look at him and sent him home again thus costing him one day's pay. Times were hard indeed and even arrival at the depot one minute late could result in similar treatment.

Another incident around this time was perhaps more amusing. During repair work it was sometimes necessary to interrupt the power supply. This came from the Aylestone Works which provided current for industry and private users alike. One Sunday morning the points were being replaced outside St Peter's church when the power was cut off for a period. This upset the vicar who came out to complain that the organ had suddenly ceased to function during the playing of the hymn 'Lead kindly light. . .'

During the 1914–1918 war many men inevitably went to serve in the forces. As a result lady conductresses were introduced although they were not allowed the responsibility of becoming drivers. The Tramway Committee issued notices asking passengers for their 'kind consideration under the new conditions'. The public were asked to have their fares ready and ask for as little change as possible. It was also agreed that soldiers and sailors in uniform could travel at half fare and evacuees to Leicester were asked 'never to ride on a bus or tram if they could possibly walk'.

At the end of the war the system, like many others, was found to be in a very run-down state. The conversion of open-topped cars to covered top had been suspended during hostilities and about half the fleet still remained to be changed. In 1919 business picked up dramatically with over 62 million passengers carried on the 160 cars now available.

Work to extend routes also went ahead including the Welford Road line to Clarendon Park which opened in 1922. The route involved a sharp curve and a steep hill and 12 cars were fitted with 'slipper' brakes as a safety precaution. Powers had been obtained to construct numerous further lines but many such ideas were shelved including a link between the Aylestone and Clarendon Park routes as well as an extension of the Belgrave route to Birstall.

During 1920 the fleet was increased by a further 18 cars, partly for use on the new Welford Road line and partly through generally increased traffic. At last the run-down state from the war was being overcome with track relaying and wire renewal. Eventually all the cars were top covered but six were never fully enclosed or vestibuled. These were withdrawn from regular service in 1933 after the closure of the Melbourne Road route but four of them came out occasionally as football specials. The purchase of further cars was considered since a number of the extensions previously approved had still not been totally abandoned. Yet they never proceeded and the fleet total (apart from water cars) never exceeded 178.

It was decided in 1922 to close the small depots at Stoneygate and Narborough Road. At the same time the permanent way stores and traffic control office in Humberstone Gate, which already accommodated 12 cars for rush-hour services, was modified to house another 13 cars and to become the Central depot. Some local residents may still recall the tight squeeze to get tramcars through the tiny hole in the wall next to the Bell Hotel and inside there were similar problems. The first car in each night had to reverse six times and negotiate as many points to reach the back of the shed.

There was much enthusiasm when in December 1923 Leicester saw its first fully enclosed tram. This was car no 86 which was rebuilt following an overhaul and top covering. The stairs were changed so that passengers could enter either saloon at the same time instead of having to jostle their way in as with all the other cars. The adapted car, which could now carry 58, was tried out for three months but any plans to convert further cars were abandoned due to the high costs involved. Since car no 86 could admit people two at the time, side by side, it acquired the nick-name of 'Noah's Ark'.

In 1924 a stretch of reserved track was laid in the centre of the twin carriageways along Blackbird Road. Sleepers were purchased from the Great Central Railway and in all the line cost over £50,000. It was provided to give an alternative outlet from the Abbey Park Road depot and an added bonus for the passengers was the provision of special circular tours on Sunday evenings at 3d (just over 1p) a time. The cars ran (weather permitting) from the Clock Tower from 5.00 pm leaving every few minutes. The last

Car 139 originated as an open-topped car. Photograph taken in London Road looking towards Granby Street and Charles Street. (Colin Withey collection)

extension to be built came in 1927 when a short branch was completed to Coleman Road off the Humberstone route. There was a proposal to extend this to a terminus at the General Hospital but this was never done.

An experiment was carried out in 1930 when three cars (145, 59 and 97) were fitted with different types of bow collectors instead of the usual trolley poles. In addition car no 42 was fitted with a pantograph the following year. The Groby Road and Blackbird Road routes had just been linked and this provided an opportunity to restring the overhead wires to take both systems. With bow collectors and pantographs the possibility of dewirement was removed and higher speeds were possible. It was also a system gaining favour elsewhere in the country and particularly on the continent but at Leicester no further conversions were carried out. Already there was talk of abandoning trams for trolleybuses or motor buses but the expense could not be justified. Instead it was decided that improvements would be made to the system incurring only moderate expense.

The first closure came in 1933 when the Melbourne Road section, linking the Eastern and Southern services, was abandoned. The track had become completely worn out and, mostly single with passing loops, replacement would have involved numerous sets of points. The councillors were again considering alternatives to the trams but had divided ideas on the subject. Quite a number preferred motor buses but those who favoured trolleybuses had of course the support of the Electricity Department. In the end it was considered that the Clock Tower area would produce such a 'forest of overhead cables' that motor buses won the vote by 21 to 14.

When the Second World War came in 1939 plans for the gradual abandonment were held in abeyance. Despite the inevitable shortage of spares, trams kept up a smart appearance on the streets. Once again conductresses were introduced to help out. Leicester was fortunate in being spared heavy bombing as had been suffered in nearby Coventry yet there were incidents. A bomb left a large hole one night near the junction of Avenue Road and London Road and there was another in East Park Road. In both instances services were speedily restored. Flashes from overhead wires presented a 'blackout' hazard and drivers were continually reminded to 'notch-off' when going through a breaker. The warnings were certainly justified for pilots flying across England reckoned they could usually tell when they were over certain towns because of this effect.

After the war the closure of the system went ahead without delay. The first to go was the Clarendon Park route via Welford Road which ceased services on 1st May 1945 and next came the Aylestone route on 5th January 1947. As time passed so the remaining lines closed one by one. The final day came on 9th November 1949 when the last car, no 58, left the Clock Tower just after 4 pm for Humberstone and then back to the Central depot.

From there it took an official party to the Abbey Park Road depot. According to the *Leicester Mercury*, the car was painted white and pale blue with flags flying from its roof. The honour of driving the last car went to Mr F Timson, the Corporation's senior tram driver, and the conductor was Mr J W Bennett. When it reached Abbey Park Road, the tram was driven by 88 year old Mr Jack White of Great Easton, Rutland, who had driven the first tram in Leicester.

For many years after the closure enthusiasts could find tram bodies at various locations. Five existed at Markfield but today, over 40 years later, they are no more since the elements have destroyed them. Two further cars in really excellent condition and complete except for trucks were until recent years on allotments at Wigston. The land was later purchased by a property developer who immediately carried out the unforgivable act of setting fire to them! One of the water cars was bought by a farmer to save himself the cost of piping and supplying water to distant isolated fields.

The Stoneygate depot is still there. For a time it served as a museum for old locomotives but these too have gone and it is now a council store. The Abbey Park Road depot is a bus depot but tram tracks can still be found in the repair shop. The reservation at Blackbird Road is also visible.

On the side of that last car which ran in November 1949 the following words had been painted in black:

> 'We mourn the loss of faithful friends
> From the streets of our grand old city.
> To move with the times, we cannot have lines
> So – Go they must – it's a pity"

Brush Electrical Engineering Co Ltd, Loughborough

Despite the existence of an extensive area of tramway track at Loughborough, eleven miles to the north of Leicester, there was never a public tramway system. It was at the famous Falcon Works that large numbers of tramcars were built for use elsewhere and the track, constructed in 1901, was used as a dual gauge (4 ft 8½ in and 3 ft 6 in) test area. It included a long branch and an artificial hill and there were also sharp curves to simulate street corners.

The Falcon Works began its existence in 1851, on land probably opposite Loughborough's Regent Street and between the A6 Derby Road and the canal. Four years later in 1855 it was taken over by Henry Hughes and by the early 1860s it became known as the 'Falcon Engine Works'. Hughes manufactured saddle tank locomotives and in 1863 he acquired the present Falcon site by Loughborough's Midland Railway station so that his locomotives could be despatched easily, without the use of road haulage.

During 1876 Hughes tried out a steam tramway locomotive on Leicester's horse tramway system. Known as 'Hughes Patent Steam Tramway Engine', it was not successful and in Leicester nothing further was heard of it. Yet Hughes was successful elsewhere, building and hiring steam locomotives with customers

including the Vale of Clyde, Paris and Bristol. The steam tram engine 'Pioneer' came from the Falcon Works, destined for the Swansea & Mumbles Railway. Another was for the Wantage Tramway (locomotive no 4) where it remained for 43 years, the longest serving UK Hughes tram engine (*Tramways Remembered – West & South West England* – chapter 14).

The Falcon company went into liquidation in 1881 to eventually become 'The Falcon Engine & Car Works Ltd' owned by Norman Russell. The construction of tram locomotives and horse cars continued – £185 per car was quoted to the London Southern Tramways Co in 1881 – and in 1885 Falcon was building its first horse buses. In 1889 the Falcon Works was taken over by the Anglo-American Brush Electric Light Corporation Ltd, to become the Brush Electrical Engineering Co Ltd. It was this take-over that set the foundation for future production lines with the bringing together of the advanced Falcon coachwork and the already proven Brush electrical equipment.

Charles Brush had come from Cleveland, Ohio, USA and, after graduating from the University of Michigan, he soon invented an arc lamp controlled by flowing current and designed and built an experimental dynamo. His fame grew and by 1877 he was developing public lighting systems. By the following year Brush was introducing similar systems in the UK and many orders followed. A company was established in Belvedere Road in Lambeth, London, and equipment was marketed on a wide scale. Paddington railway station was supplied with Brush lighting.

Following the 1889 take-over of the Falcon Works, the heavy equipment at Lambeth was moved to Loughborough and many

Lambeth workers moved to the area with their families. The following year the Brush works in Cleveland was bought by Thompson Houston. The UK company went from strength to strength and already Brush was considering new systems to apply electricity for urban tramways. One of the pioneers was Emil Garcke who for many years had thought, not only of electrifying tramways in the cities, but also going on to networks of interurban systems. By 1894 Brush was producing tramcars at the rate of 250 a year and, in 1895, Garcke, as Brush's managing director, set up the British Electric Traction Co (BET) as a pioneer company.

By the turn of the century the tramcar business was booming. In 1900 Manchester ordered 200 cars, the company's largest order yet. During the period 1901 to 1906 further orders flooded in. Tramcars were ordered for Chesterfield and for Derby, for the Burton and Ashby Light Railway and for the Mansfield & District Light Railway. At the same time Brush built all the steel rolling stock for the underground railways. In 1911 Emil Garcke became company chairman and in the same year the London County Council ordered 200 tramcars. By the mid-1920s many towns were considering motor buses as an alternative transport system and here too Brush was successful. When Leicester Corporation commenced motor bus services, the buses had bodies made by Brush. During 1930/31, Brush received its last big order for tramcars – approximately 100 for Leeds. Brush's last order for trams came in 1937 being Blackpool cars 284–303 built in 1937.

Brush has of course prospered over the years to become today part of the vast and successful Hawker Siddeley group. British Rail's powerful type 4 diesel-electric main-line locomotive (BR class 47) introduced in 1962 is probably one of their best known products in today's Britain. Yet the town of Loughborough nearly had its own public tramway system. In 1901 the Loughborough & District Electric Traction Syndicate Ltd received powers to build 6½ miles of 3 ft 6 in gauge track from Loughborough via Quorndon to Mountsorrel with three short branches in the town. The line never came about yet had it been built (and had a 4 ft 8½ in gauge been chosen) then trams would have reached more than half way to link with those from Leicester.

Chapter 15

A SURFACE CONTACT SYSTEM IN LINCOLNSHIRE

(Lincoln Tramway Co Ltd and City of Lincoln Tramways)

Lincoln Tramway Co Ltd

Lincoln's first public transport began in 1880 when horse-drawn buses provided a service between the city centre and Bracebridge. It was run by a firm called Jackson & Son but, two years later, the Lincoln Tramway Company was formed to cover more or less the same route. A 3 ft 6 in gauge track was laid and a fleet of eight horse-drawn trams was purchased. These comprised six one-horse single-decker saloons and two open cars, popularly known as 'toast racks', for the summer service. The 1¾ mile journey from The Gatehouse Hotel at Bracebridge to St Benedict's Square usually took 20 minutes although level crossings often caused delays.

Timekeeping was generally good and it was reckoned the horses could keep up a steady trot. The trams were one-horse vehicles

Electric car no 1 leaves the High Street for Bracebridge c1906. The service began on 23rd November 1905 and in the first eleven days over 40,000 passengers were carried. (Lens of Sutton)

although in bad weather two horses were yoked up. The passengers had quite an affection for the animals and often fed them tit-bits along the route. It was considered the animals were quite intelligent too. With normal loads, the horses did three journeys before being rested and, when it was time to be relieved, the horses would turn their heads as they passed the Ellison Street depot to see if the relief was there!

The journey into the city was covered in two stages of one penny (less than ½p), the intermediate point being Cranwell House near St Botolphs church. The service was rather infrequent with a first car leaving Bracebridge at 5.30 am, with two more in the morning, three in the afternoon and three in the evening. There were extra journeys on Fridays and Saturdays. In August 1901 a half-penny fare for workmen was introduced and in the first few months over 7,000 used this service. This move helped the company to make a profit during 1901 of £763 9s 10d (just under £763.50) during which period 938,520 passengers were carried.

The Lincoln Tramway Company remained independent until 1902 when it was taken over by the Lincoln Corporation at a purchase price of £10,488 with the intention that it should be converted to an electric powered system. The last horse tram ran on 22nd July 1905 from St Benedict's Square to Bracebridge. The cars usually seated around 20 passengers but on this occasion there were 80 aboard. The horse was decorated for the occasion and thousands of people turned out to witness the event.

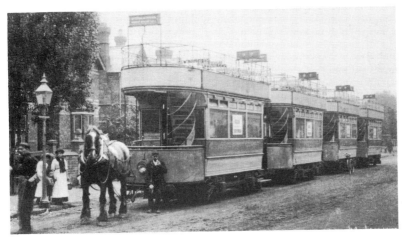

Four new electric cars arrive at Lincoln from Brush at Loughborough in 1905 and each awaits delivery by horse to the depot at Bracebridge where final assembly will be completed. (Lens of Sutton)

Trams were frequently delayed by level crossings – this one adjacent to the Great Northern Railway station. Note the semaphore signal to the right, used to control the trams. (Lens of Sutton)

Three days later the cars were sold at an auction, realising between £3 10s (£3.50) and £6 5s (£6.25) each. Many were used locally as summerhouses and one spent many years in the garden of the Gatehouse Hotel close to the Bracebridge terminus. The horses realised a total of 450 guineas (£472.50) and one was bought by a cabby from Nottingham. It was said he was eventually forced to resell, because each time he crossed tram tracks in Nottingham, the horse would turn and follow the rails!

City of Lincoln Tramways
Lincoln's electric tramway system was one of the shortest public undertakings built in the UK. Cars ran from St Benedict's Square to the junction of Maple Street and Newark Road in Bracebridge. Other routes had been proposed but none of these materialised. It was suggested that trams might leave St Catherines to travel along South Park and Canwick Road to Broadgate where tracks would separate to Old Barracks in Burton Road, Newport Road and also along Monks Road. Yet only the stretch of just under two miles was ever constructed.

The system was unique too, since Lincoln was the first to use the Griffith-Bedell surface contact stud system. It was chosen to avoid the use of 'unsightly poles' which would have been needed to carry the usual overhead wires. The contact 'studs' were set at intervals of 6 ft between the tracks, each containing a plunger in contact with a buried cable. With the plunger in its lower or rest position, the stud was 'dead'. Under each car was a 'skate' containing a series of magnets and just long enough to span two studs. As a car passed over a stud, the magnet lifted the plunger and made electrical contact so that current was passed to the car. Once the car had passed the stud, the plunger dropped and the stud was dead again.

122

Initially eight double-deck trams were supplied by the Brush Electric Company of Loughborough, the first six being open top deck type each powered by two 25 hp motors. Nos 7 and 8 were fitted with covered top decks and open canopies powered by two 35 hp motors. The cars had to be fitted with the necessary equipment to work on the stud system and this work was carried out at the Bracebridge depot. The first car completed was no 6 which was sent out on test runs on 29th October 1905 when a section of track was ready and also converted from 3 ft 6 in to 4 ft 8½ in gauge. A trial with members of the corporation as passengers held on 11th November proved successful but only, according to a local press report, because engineers had taken the car out around midnight the previous night 'on the quiet' to check faults in the studs.

The official opening ceremony came on 23rd November 1905 when car no 1, suitably decorated with bunting, covered the route loaded to capacity with civic dignitaries and many other influential people. The driver was Mr E H Curtis who later became Chief Inspector and who had come to Lincoln from Leeds where he had gained considerable experience on trams. Public services followed immediately and over 40,000 passengers were carried in the first eleven days of operation. Many compliments were paid to the corporation for adopting a system without overhead wires.

During 1907 and 1908 four of the open-top cars were provided with top covers supplied by Milnes Voss. For the present, all cars retained their open drivers' platforms leaving motormen exposed to all weathers. Yet the Lincoln system could claim another unique aspect, for each side of the Great Northern Railway level crossing trams obeyed railway type semaphore signals. In addition there were catchpoints each side of the crossing operated by the railway signalmen and designed to derail a car if it overran when approaching closed gates.

In theory the stud system was good but in practice it gave a lot of

The level crossing, photographed in October 1990, still delays traffic near the city centre but the trams went over 60 years ago. (Author)

problems. Sometimes the plunger failed to fall after a car had left it, leaving it live. Only too often there was a fatal result when a horse happened to cross the tracks. Alternatively a stud could stick in the down position, particularly in frosty or snowy weather. A tram could often coast over a dead stud but, should a car happen to stop, it was not so easy. Often the motorman and conductor had the task of using a crowbar on the spokes of the car's wheels to move the car on. Also it was not possible to inserts studs at points, cross-overs and level crossings so power was lost and cars had to coast. This also meant of course that at night all the car's lights went out.

During the 1914–1918 war, faults became more frequent as parts and labour became more scarce. At the same time the demand for transport increased particularly with a munitions drive in the local works. New cars were unobtainable and second-hand cars could not be found. An improvement was obtained in April 1918 when two ex-horse trailer cars were purchased from the Great Grimsby Street Tramways Company for £120, these serving until 1921. After the war, conversion to overhead wires became inevitable and, after this had taken place in December 1919, there was very little further trouble. With the conversion came three new cars (9–11) from the English Electric Co Ltd making a total fleet of eleven cars during the system's life. Although the English Electric cars were faster (each had two 40 hp motors), the seating upstairs was not so comfortable. There were complaints that when two people sat on a double seat, one could only occupy the seat with 'overhang'.

Just before Christmas 1919 the trolley reverser at St Benedict's Square caused one of its biggest traffic jams ever. Car no 9 was

Car no 6 bound for Bracebridge along Lincoln's High Street in 1923. The following year this car was totally enclosed for £111. But it was considered expensive and the remainder of the fleet did not follow although all cars did have their driver's platforms enclosed. (Pamlin Prints)

leaving when the trolley left the wire and shot up into a nearly vertical position. Normally the trolley could be retrieved with the hooked-end pole carried on the side of the tram but in this instance electric wires were in the way. Unfortunately no crowbar was available to move the tram so a 'stud' car was brought in to help. This moved slowly into a 'pushing' position and then met a 'dead' stud' Two immovable cars now blocked the High Street. A crowbar was eventually found but meantime the crowds which had turned out to watch rivalled those of Armistice Night. The folk of Lincoln never thought they would ever again see such a traffic jam!

The drivers were still exposed to all weathers and in 1924 the corporation decided experimentally to fully enclose the ends of both decks of car no 6. This was carried out at a cost of £111 producing what was described as 'a remarkably handsome car'. Unfortunately it was thought the cost was too great so no others were converted, although all the cars did have their driver's

When visited in October 1990, the tram depot at Bracebridge, previously a car showroom, was up for sale. Note the four supports above the front windows which carried the overhead wires into the building. Inside it was still possible to determine the 'filled-in' tracks. (Author)

The remains of Lincoln's tram body no 3 in a private garden at Waddington. The owners of the property (aged 89 and 90) clearly recalled the days when travelling in such a tram. (Author)

platforms enclosed. Possibly the corporation were considering the tramway's future for since 1920 a service of petrol buses had been operating elsewhere in the city. When in 1925, buses began working the Bracebridge route on Sundays, it was considered to be the thin end of the wedge towards an all bus system.

The fate of Lincoln's trams was sealed when the first Leyland double-decker bus was purchased in 1927 and a large bus garage opened in 1928. By early 1929 there were sufficient double-decker buses to allow closure of the tramway system and this was fixed for 4th March 1929. The last car, no 6, was suitably decorated and left St Benedict's Square at 3 pm on Monday, 4th March 1929. It was preceded by most of the other cars loaded to capacity in what was described as 'a melancholy procession to the depot'. A report in *The Lincolnshire Chronicle* suggested that the conductors of Lincoln's trams never need fear unemployment. Bearing in mind their past achievements in carrying so many passengers for each load, they would surely qualify for work such as sardine packers.

Many of the cars were sold but cars 9, 10 and 11 went to Preston Corporation to become 13, 18 and 22, bought for £1823 each and each sold for £675. They were scrapped when its system closed down. Today the depot at Bracebridge is still there opposite the local library. When visited in October 1990, the filled-in tracks could be determined and the supports over the doorways which carried the overhead wires were still there.

One Lincoln electric tram body has survived the years. Located in a front garden at Waddington (on strictly private property), it stands resplendent overlooking a lawn yet somewhat the worse for wear. It is the body of tram no 3 and the owners of the property (aged 89 and 90!) recalled when it was originally acquired in 1929 by their uncle – and very much against the family's wishes. It was delivered to its present 'resting place' by the local blacksmith's horse and cart. For a time it was used to keep poultry but subsequently it has served as a 'pavilion' for occasional tennis parties – and even a venue for the members of Waddington Parish Church choir.

Chapter 16

TRAMS ALONG THE HUMBER

(Trams in Grimsby and Cleethorpes and the Grimsby &
Immingham Electric Railway)

*Great Grimsby Street Tramways Company, Grimsby Corporation
Tramways and Cleethorpes Corporation Tramways*

Saturday, 4th June 1881, was a gloriously sunny day in the fishing
town of Grimsby and it seemed that the whole population turned
out to cheer the town's first public transport service. Negotiations
had begun in 1876 with the Portsmouth based Provincial Tramway
Company seeing Grimsby as a growing fishing port and also
providing an opportunity to expand its own tramway system.
Finally in 1879, Parliament agreed the construction of two routes.

The horse trams proved an immediate success. A depot was
built in Park Street and trams proceeded along Cleethorpe Road to
Riby Square. One route took trams down Victoria Street to finish
at Bargate opposite the Wheatsheaf and another went along Freeman Street to finish at a junction with Welholme Road. The fare at
the time was considered good value at 1d (less than ½p) to
anywhere in the borough. The trams operated under the name of
The Great Grimsby Street Tramway Company, which was a
subsidiary of the Portsmouth company.

Electric trams came to Grimsby and Cleethorpes on 7th December 1901. The gauge was 4 ft 8½ ins and current collection
was by overhead wire. Trams ran from the People's Park in

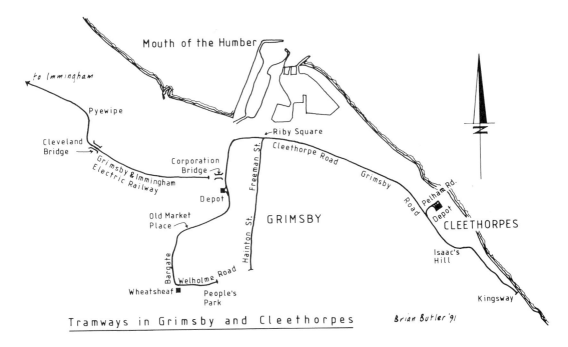

Tramways in Grimsby and Cleethorpes   *Brian Butler '91*

Great Grimsby Street Tramways horse car no 11 at the entrance to the Park Street depot. After electrification, this car was kept for use as a trailer, mainly for football traffic. It was sold to Lincoln Corporation in 1918. (Photo: Humberside County Libraries)

Welholme Road via Riby Square to Kingsway in Cleethorpes. A reserved track extension along the Kingsway was authorised but, due to a disagreement over fares to be charged, it was never completed. Only the first few yards were built. In Grimsby, a second route took trams down Freeman Street and Hainton Street but the Great Northern Railway would not allow trams over its level crossing for the route to link with the People's Park terminus.

A new depot was built in Pelham Road, Cleethorpes, where today there is a fish processing centre. A number of the horse trams were retained and these were kept for use as trailers, particularly on the 'football specials'. Two of these trailers were sold to Lincoln Corporation Tramways in 1918. The original Park Street depot became a skating rink and, later on, the Strand Cinema. The Strand was a popular place but the building was lost during bombing in World War II. After the war, the site was occupied by a block of flats.

The electric tramway system began with 24 open-top four-wheeled cars supplied by Dick, Kerr & Co Ltd of Preston. Seating in the lower saloon was longitudinal whilst on top there were reversible garden seats. The cars were painted a basic green and cream and they carried fancy iron scrollwork. The title Great Grimsby Street Tramways appeared on the rocker panels. In 1904 three cars were fitted with enclosed top covers although these were later altered to open balcony. In the same year, four cars acquired

Car no 14 in Grimsby's Market Place c1910. Electric trams came to Grimsby in December 1901 with certain routes surviving until 1937 when replaced by trolleybuses. (Lens of Sutton)

from the Alexandra Park Electric Railway in North London when it closed in 1899, were rebuilt as double-deckers. They had originated as single-deck cars built in 1898 in Germany.

In his book, *Memories of Grimsby and Cleethorpes Transport*, the late W H Lucas wrote of an amusing incident experienced by one of the early tram drivers. He was about to descend Isaac's Hill in Cleethorpes when the trolley pole became de-wired and the head, which was detachable, was catapulted away. The driver and conductor searched everywhere, even in the nearby front gardens, but without success. The incident had to be reported to the general manager who told the driver that the trolley head had to be found and that the driver should not come back until it was.

Two days were spent at the scene – but no trolley head was found. On the third day the driver noticed a nearby house had damaged slates on the roof. He knocked the door and asked the lady of the house if he might be allowed to climb into her roof. There the search ended with the trolley head found lying on the wooden framework of the ceiling. The manager was satisfied and the driver kept his job.

By 1918 the fleet comprised 31 cars plus numerous trailers. In 1922 a novel open single-deck touring car (no 40) was built, capable of seating 40 passengers. This was similar in appearance to the motor charabancs which could be seen operating from the seafront at Cleethorpes. The car lasted three years, to be sold in 1925 to the Portsmouth & Horndean Light Railway.

Also in 1925, on 6th April, and after lengthy legal procedures, Grimsby Corporation acquired the lines within its own area. Many of the cars were by now in very poor condition and a number had to be withdrawn. Their places were taken by 16 Brush cars built in 1913 and purchased from Sunderland District Electric Tramways Co Ltd. The Great Grimsby Street Tramways vehicles continued to ply between Park Street and Kingsway and, with through services continuing to operate, it became a common sight to see Grimsby's trams in Cleethorpes.

Gradual conversion from trams to trolleybuses began in

129

Grimsby. On 3rd October 1926, single-deck trolleybuses not only took over the section down Freeman Street and Hainton Avenue but extended it to the junction with Weelsby Road. Conversion on other routes followed although the section from Riby Square to Park Street continuing to Cleethorpes survived until the end of March 1937. In July 1936, Cleethorpes Urban District Council purchased the route within its area and, twelve months later, proceeded with trolleybus conversion. During that twelve months Cleethorpes became a borough so the tramway had two owners in quick succession. First came the 'Cleethorpes UDC Tramways Dept', then 'Cleethorpes Corporation Tramways Dept'. On 17th July 1937 trams in Cleethorpes came to an end with trolleybuses taking over completely. Thirty six years of electric trams in Grimsby and Cleethorpes had come to an end.

Grimsby & Immingham Electric Railway

In May 1912 the Great Central Railway (GCR) opened a 5¾ mile long electric tramway between Grimsby and a new dock being completed at Immingham. Since January 1910 the GCR had been

Grimsby Corporation Tramways depot in Victoria Street still carrying the date 1925. The building was originally a seaplane hangar from Killingholme dating back to 1912. (Colin Withey collection)

The Victoria Street depot today serves the town's buses but the tram tracks can still be found inside – much to the bus crews' annoyance! The walls and frontage are still the same but the roof has been rebuilt. (Author)

operating a steam rail motor service between Grimsby (Pyewipe Road) and Immingham Halt, but it was proving hardly adequate and, to make matters worse, no direct road access was possible over the marshland between the dwelling houses of Grimsby and the new port complex. An improved transport system was therefore considered essential.

Services along the 4 ft 8½ ins gauge Grimsby & Immingham Electric Railway (G&IER) began on Wednesday, 15th May 1912. Initially the route was from Grimsby (Corporation Bridge) on street track to the depot at Pyewipe, from where a straight single line with passing loops was laid as traditional railway track to Immingham Halt. There was no opening ceremony when the trams began because a Royal opening was planned for Immingham Dock during the summer. Despite the lack of celebration, hundreds of passengers travelled on the new cars on the first day – so many in fact that the conductor ran out of through tickets! During the following weekend, thousands more made the trip.

The first eight cars came from the Brush Electrical Engineering Co of Loughborough and four of these were, without doubt, the longest in Britain. To be used for workmen's services, they were over 54 ft long, each seated 64 passengers and each was powered by two 50 hp Dick, Kerr motors. The other four were smaller cars, 38 ft 10 ins long, required for normal service. All cars had a central luggage compartment which had double doors each side and which added a further eight seats. According to J H Price, writing on The Grimsby & Immingham Railway in *Tramway Review*, these compartments were soon to attract groups of regulars playing at cards who resented any invasion of their privacy. The compartments came to be known locally as 'horse boxes' although there is no record of them being used in such a way.

The Royal visit to open Immingham Dock came on Monday, 22nd July 1912, when King George V and Queen Mary arrived by Royal train to be greeted by some 2,000 official guests who had travelled by special GCR trains from many parts of the country.

Grimsby car no 39 in Old Market Place. This car was built at Grimsby in 1925 and received its balcony top cover the following year. (Photo: Humberside County Libraries)

After a celebratory lunch and a visit aboard the new GCR paddle steamer *SS Killingholme*, the King pressed a button and Immingham Docks inner lock gates officially opened. Speeches followed and at 3.30 pm the Royal Train left for London. There had been many onlookers and, when they returned to Grimsby on the trams, the line experienced one of its busiest days.

In 1913, the necessary extension from Immingham Halt to the Dock terminus was completed giving a total route of almost seven miles. This involved a trailing junction in the road at Immingham Town which meant that cars had to reverse to cross over the freight railway on the road bridge. A reserved roadside track took trams to a terminus close to the Dock offices. The section opened on Monday, 17th November, with cars from Grimsby's Corporation Bridge leaving every 20 minutes with a running time of 27 minutes. Dockers and railwaymen were the main clientele, the latter travelling free!

Four more 64-seater cars were required in March 1914 by the G&IER but the price from Brush had risen to £1266 each and was considered too expensive. The work was therefore given to the GCR's own carriageworks at Dukinfield which in 1915 produced cars 13–16. In July of the same year, a half-mile section of single track constructed along Queens Road towards Immingham village, was inspected and agreed by the Board of Trade but it never opened to traffic. Its purpose could well have been the start of a line to Habrough or a possible link with a proposed tramway (which never developed) between Barton (for ferries to Hull) and Immingham. It had been built following pressure from Grimsby Council which had pointed out such a line was included in a 1908 agreement and the G&IER therefore became legally obliged to

Grimsby Corporation tramcar no 46 c1930. This was one of 16 cars originally built in 1913 by Brush and bought second-hand from Sunderland District Electric Tramways to replace the aging ex-company cars. (Colin Withey collection)

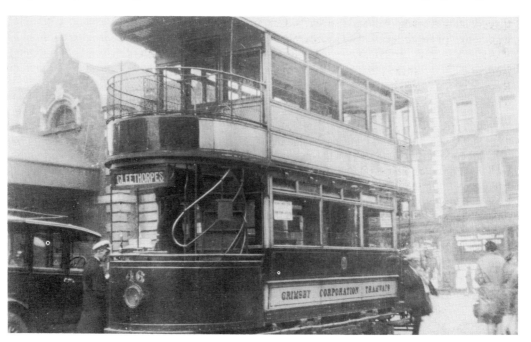

A 64-seater single-deck tramcar in LNER days at the Grimsby & Immingham Electric Railway. This was one of twelve similar cars, said to be the longest in the country. (Photo: Humberside County Libraries)

build it. Apart from the running of a franchise car once every three months, it was never used.

In January 1923 the GCR became part of the London & North Eastern Railway (LNER). During the 1920s many cruise liners serving the Norwegian Fjords brought the tramway extra business. Regular boat trains arrived from London and passengers could also be issued with through tickets on the trams. For a number of years powers had been held by the GCR and LNER to lay tracks across Corporation Bridge to link with the town's tramways but this was never carried out and the powers lapsed in 1931.

During the Second World War there was concern over the possibility of flashes from the trolley wheels being seen by German aircraft or submarines. In 1940 the trolley wheels were replaced by swivelling carbon shoes known by the men as 'carbon runners'. During the night of 18/19th January 1941, there was a different sort of hazard. Heavy snow halted all the cars along the line and three had to be dug out of snowdrifts. On future occasions the line was better prepared, utilising a snowplough to keep the track clear.

After the war, on 1st January 1948, the railways were nationalised and the tramway became part of British Railways (Eastern Region). By now the track within Corporation Road was badly worn and cars could be heard over quite a distance. It was claimed that many nearby residents had no need for alarm clocks! In addition to this, rail-joint noises could also be heard and it was for this reason the tramway acquired the nickname 'The Clickety-Clack'. Track renewal was discussed but shelved, since discussions were taking place over possible abandonment with replacement by buses. During 1955 over one million passengers were carried, yet despite this BR later claimed that the line was 'an absolute dead loss'. Rolling stock was in a poor condition and in very short supply and to overcome this, 19 high-capacity front-exit single-deck cars were bought from the Gateshead & District Tramways when that system closed in August 1951. Three of these were already secondhand from Newcastle Corporation.

During 1955, after much negotiation, BR offered the 1¼ mile section of line within the Grimsby area to the council free-of-

Grimsby & Immingham car no 20 at the National Tramway Museum at Crich prior to resuming its original identity as Gateshead car no 5. This 48-seater car, built in 1927, was loaned by the museum during 1990 to the Gateshead Garden Festival. (Lens of Sutton)

charge. The council accepted and, after protracted union opposition, it closed on 30th June 1956 to be replaced by corporation buses. Trams now terminated at Cleveland Bridge (Pyewipe) and the journey time to Immingham Dock was 19 minutes. In 1958 BR made it clear to various local employers that the tramway would be closed if they could not offer financial help. This was refused and BR gave notice it intended to apply for permission to close the line. Petitions against closure were organised and a meeting of the Transport Users' Consultative Committee (TUCC) was held at Grimsby to hear objections. A compromise resulted with trams run at peak times and buses for the remainder of the day on a circuitous route.

It was soon clear the buses were carrying many more fare-paying passengers than the trams so in December 1960 BR again applied for closure. BR said that if it was refused it would consider running diesel trains to replace the trams. The council saw this as a threat to its bus revenue so support to BR closure was given. The TUCC met again and this time BR's application was successful. When the last official car, no 4, made its journey, it was carrying boards reading, 'Grimsby-Immingham Electric Railway. Last Day. 1st July 1961'. According to the *Evening Telegraph*, the driver, Frank Jewitt, recalled that one night he counted 151 passengers on board – more standing than sitting and some even riding on the 'buffers'. He maintained it was a shame to close the line. It was a sad day for many.

The Grimsby & Immingham tramway office can still be found in Corporation Road although the station itself has long since gone. Since closure, the office has served as a cafe, a saddlery and a chandlery. The Immingham Museum in Waterworks Lane at Immingham is also well worth a visit. Recollections of the tramway include pictures and models and also a reversible wooden seat from one of the original cars restored by the museum in 1986.

In addition three tramcars have survived and two of these can be found at the National Tramway Museum at Crich. When visited in

The Grimsby & Immingham tramway closed in July 1961 and tramcar no 14, seen here at Crich in October 1990, is one of the three survivors. The car had been repainted and varnished but it is not currently operational. (Author)

All that remains of the Grimsby & Immingham tramway office serving in October 1990 as a chandlery. The station had long since been demolished. There were plans that the trams should link with the town's system by crossing Corporation Bridge (seen far right) but this never happened. (Author)

October 1990, the 64-seater car no 14 had been repainted in BR electric multiple unit green and varnished to good effect but it was not operational. The second was car no 20 which had assumed its original identity as Gateshead 5. This shorter 48-seater car was in working order but loaned to work the tram service within the 1990 Gateshead Garden Festival grounds. A third car, no 26, was acquired by The North of England Open Air Museum at Beamish in 1968 after a period in store. Restoration to its initial Gateshead condition as car no 10, was completed in 1973, making possible the inauguration of the Beamish tramway.

A unique aspect of the Grimsby & Immingham Electric Railway was that it was a British Rail passenger service operating a regular 24 hour service – a feature not again equalled until the arrival of the Gatwick Express many years later.

Chapter 17

The End of the Trams. . .

The decline of the tram was as dramatic as its development. The first electric system to fail in the Eastern Counties was at Ipswich, one of the first towns in the country to convert a route from tram to trolleybus operation. Three Railless/English Electric Company vehicles began services in September 1923 and, within almost three years, the trolleybuses (known locally as 'trackless trams') had taken over. A further three years later, in 1929, the small tramway systems in Lincoln and Colchester gave way to motor bus services.

The first system to be abandoned in the 1930s was at Peterborough where, once again, motor buses took over. Yet despite the trams' 27 years of faithful service to the town's citizens, the local press unkindly commented, 'Their death has been long and lingering, but none the less slow but sure, to the great relief of all concerned.' Over the next five years, more towns bade farewell to the trams. First at Lowestoft, then at Luton and Great Yarmouth, then at Northampton. At Norwich, on 10th December 1935, it seemed the crowds that turned out to watch the closure were even greater than when services had begun 35 years earlier.

Trams failed for a number of financial and political reasons. Municipalities generally underestimated the length of life of the vehicles and they had little experience of providing for obsolescence. Track repairs also became a financial problem. Tracks usually lasted about 15 to 20 years but often any allowance made for this had been spent on more essential work on the tramway, especially after the effects of the 1914–1918 war. In the 1930s trams just went out of fashion following the publicity given to the first really reliable and passenger-friendly buses. The inability of management in some instances to provide through services proved another weakness, as did the cost of extending the tramlines as towns rapidly grew in the 1920s and 1930s. As a unit of transport the tram was uneconomic in the areas of low population found on a town's outskirts. Overall in the relatively lowly populated towns of the Eastern Counties, bus economics were clearly superior.

Tramways in Britain reached a peak in 1919–1920 with an annual total of 4,800 million passengers carried. Discounting the year of the General Strike, figures kept high, falling to only 4,700 million by 1927–1928. Route mileage in 1913 was 2,530, reaching its peak of 2,624 eleven years later in 1924. But by the early 1930s only 1,861 miles of track remained in service, and the rolling stock was down to 12,275 cars from a maximum of 14,000.

The Tramway Act, agreed by Parliament in 1870, initially brought about many road improvements at no cost to the local ratepayer but it proved a burden to the tramway companies. The Act originated from the days of the horse-trams, when horses would wear out the road surface and tramway undertakings were committed to the cost of paving and repairing the roadway between the rails and 18 ins outside the track. This caused much aggravation in later years when the volume and weight of motor transport produced greater wear and tear on road surfaces than ever envisaged when the tramways were built. A further costly problem was the assessment of tram tracks at their full value for local rating purposes – a particular blow to company-owned systems where hard cash had to be paid as opposed to internal paper transfer of cost between municipal departments.

As mentioned above, the tramway systems suffered during the First World War with lack of repairs and severe shortages of materials. At the same time, trams were more heavily used – many carrying workers engaged on war work. After the war their popularity increased but the role of the motor vehicle in road transport was increasing and the motor bus becoming more reliable. In some parts of the country, the trolleybus, inheriting the ruggedness and the reliability of the tramcar, was growing in importance.

When the last official tramcar made its journey between Grimsby and Immingham on 1st July 1961, it was the end of regular public services in the Eastern Counties. As the driver stepped down from his platform, he said, 'Well, that's it. The very end'.

. . . Or the beginning?
When the crowds attending the many tramway 'last nights' sang 'will ye no come back again?', they little realised that around half a century later many of their dreams could come true. Following closures, tramlines were torn up because the systems were considered outmoded, inefficient and an impediment to the growing volume of motor traffic. Yet today, as society has come to recognise more the nuisance of motor vehicles in the environment and their congestion of our towns and cities across the country, trams are seen as an alternative public transport system of the future.

In the north-east of England, the story of the tram has turned full circle. In 1904, competition from electric trams made the North Eastern Railway decide to electrify its Tyneside lines. Sixty years later, British Railways scrapped the system and replaced the electric trains with diesels. Today, the lines, now light rail, are once more electrified, modernised, extended and renamed the Tyne and Wear Metro under local ownership.

To the European visitor, the new 'trains' are immediately recognisable as British versions of the standard European trams. Blackpool no longer has the perceived monopoly on regular tram services on mainland Britain. The success of the Tyne and Wear Metro as well as London's Docklands Light Railway brought about a flood of proposals to build new tramways elsewhere. Now that the first tram has travelled on Manchester's Metrolink network and the South Yorkshire Supertram link is under construction, and with the Midland Metro in Birmingham awaiting funding, others like Nottingham now have Bills before Parliament. But far more are in the planning stage.

At the time of writing this book, numerous proposals are being put forward for light rail or tram networks in the Eastern Counties. Between Luton and Dunstable the former railway track survived to give cement and oil trains access to private sidings at Dunstable. Plans have been put forward with local backing for a light railway along this section using single-coach railbuses during peakhours. British Rail in February 1989 said that if a rail link went ahead then 'heavy' electric trains would be favoured giving a possible full service between Dunstable, Luton and London. In early 1991 transport chiefs were considering conversion of the disused line into a bus-only road but this caused concern in Dunstable where people thought the rail link might be lost for ever. Another view expressed foresaw a tramway system giving an 11-station line between Dunstable, Luton and Luton Airport. On the airport section, existing highways would be used. A final decision has still to be made, a factor very much dependent upon the availability of finance. At nearby Milton Keynes, the new town founded in 1967, the council has commissioned a feasibility study into the possibility of a rapid transit system linking the town centre with Bletchley, Newport Pagnell, Wolverton and Stony Stratford. Where housing near the town centre might make this impractical, then a partially elevated system may be considered.

East Anglia also has its share of proposals. One of these is consideration for a rapid transit (or possibly 'monorail') system at Chelmsford, also serving North Springfield and the Widford Industrial area. Another at Great Yarmouth (which lost its trams in 1933) is for a 2.5 km four-station monorail system elevated to a minimum height of 3.5 metres, mostly above public highways. Unhappily for the promoters, Norfolk County Council objected to this at the outline planning application stage. Norwich, a city certainly suffering from traffic strangulation, has numerous options under consideration. The part-use of former railway lines is a possibility – northwards towards Drayton and southwards to Lakenham. Linking with BR's Thorpe station, street running is also proposed plus the opening of five new stations with 'park and ride' facilities. A final strategy remains to be resolved.

Cambridge, which never progressed beyond horse trams, would prove unique if electric trams materialised. It would be the first time electric traction came to the city's streets. A number of proposals have been put forward and a recent feasibility study suggested a 15 km north-south line from Oakington to Trumpington (the latter connecting with the M11) with 'park and ride' facilities at each terminus. Much of the line would be along redundant railway track but there would be street-running across the city, via Newmarket Road, Emmanuel Road and Hills Road. Consultants have costed such a project at around £68 million. The council would find it difficult to fund its share and it has been suggested that one means of raising money could be by charging car-owners for the use of busy streets. Local industry too has been canvassed for support but there is opposition from the local bus company which is pursuing a policy of promoting improved services. It is pressing for bus priority as well as 'park and ride' schemes as an alternative to a light rail system.

Leicester, like Cambridge, also has a disused railway track, a former route between Birstall in the north (linking with the pre-served Great Central Railway) and Narborough in the south (close to the M1). Such a line, if developed as light rapid transit, would pass close to the centre of Leicester and allow numerous 'park and ride' facilities plus the possibility of an on-street section to the town centre. Consultants have considered such a possibility, but have concluded for the present it would be too expensive to be achieved in a reasonable time scale.

There is however encouraging news over a scheme to re-introduce passenger services between Loughborough, Leicester, Burton-upon-Trent and Derby. Although not light rapid transit, an hourly service of Sprinter trains is envisaged and considerable interest has been shown by the relevant County Councils as well as much encouragement from the private sector. Numerous new stations are proposed and it is anticipated that up to 1.8 million passengers might be carried annually. Costs are put at up to £15 million but following a Government grant agreed in early January 1992, Leicester County Council plan to have a service operational in stages in 1994 and 1995. It will become known as The Ivanhoe Line, named after Sir Walter Scott's famous novel *Ivanhoe* which was centred on the castle at Ashby de la Zouche.

For the tram enthusiast these are truly exciting times. Yet such enthusiasm must be tempered with reality, for many of the proposals are in very early stages. These various schemes will involve millions of pounds which the promoter must fund from either the public or the private sector. Government grants cannot be sought unless non-user benefit can be shown and private developers naturally look for a return from their investments. When recession is strong and the property market is weak then potential spin-off benefits may not be realised. With high interest rates, financing could prove prohibitive. Yet, as our towns become more and more congested, it is inevitable that alternative transport systems must come about. Failure to do so will surely lead to our town centres coming to an eventual complete traffic standstill when the country comes out of recession.

How those early tramway engineers would have laughed into their oily overalls!

OPENING AND FINAL CLOSURE DATES OF REGULAR PASSENGER TRAM SERVICES

Location	Initial Opening Date	Final Closure to Electric Traction
Horse and Steam Traction		
Leicester	24 Dec 1874	Oct 1904
Great Yarmouth	1 Apr 1875	4 Jul 1905
Ipswich	13 Oct 1880	6 Jun 1903
Cambridge	28 Oct 1880	18 Feb 1914 *1
Northampton	4 Jun 1881	19 Aug 1904
Grimsby/Cleethorpes	4 Jun 1881	6 Dec 1901
Lincoln	1882	22 Jul 1905
Wisbech & Upwell	20 Aug 1883	1 Jan 1928 *2
Alford & Sutton	2 Apr 1884	1 Dec 1889 *2
Wolverton & Stony Stratford	27 May 1887	4 May 1926 *2
Canvey Island (monorail)	1901	1904 *1

*1 Horse trams only
*2 Steam trams only

	Initial Opening Date	Final Closure
Electric Traction		
Norwich	30 Jul 1900	10 Dec 1935
Southend-on-Sea	19 Jul 1901	8 Apr 1942
Great Grimsby Street Tramway Company	7 Dec 1901	14 Jul 1936 *3
Great Yarmouth	19 Jun 1902	14 Dec 1933
Peterborough	24 Jan 1903	15 Nov 1930
Lowestoft	22 Jul 1903	8 May 1931
Ipswich	23 Nov 1903	26 Jul 1926
Leicester	18 May 1904	9 Nov 1949
Northampton	21 Jly 1904	15 Dec 1934
Colchester	28 Jul 1904	8 Dec 1929
Lincoln	23 Nov 1905	4 Mar 1929
Luton	21 Feb 1908	16 Apr 1932
Grimsby & Immingham Electric Railway	15 May 1912	1 Jul 1961
Grimsby Corporation	6 Apr 1925	31 Mar 1937 *3
Cleethorpes Council/Cleethorpes Corporation Tramways	15 Jul 1936	17 Jul 1937 *3

*3 In April 1925, Grimsby Corporation took over The Great Grimsby Street Tramway Company within its boundaries. Cleethorpes took similar action in July 1936.

BIBLIOGRAPHY

I have referred to numerous sources (many of which are no longer in print) which include the following and can be recommended for further reading:

Charles Klapper	The Golden Age of Tramways	Routledge & Kegan Paul
R C Anderson	The Tramways of East Anglia	Light Rail Transit Association
R C Anderson and J C Gillham	The Tramways of East Anglia	Light Rail Transit Association
V E Burrows	The Tramways of Southend-on-Sea	Advertiser Press Ltd
Peggy Dowie and Ken Crowe	A Century of Iron – A History of Southend's Iron Pier	Friends of Southend Pier Museum
K Turner	Pier Railways	Oakwood Press
Colchester Corporation Transport, 1904–1964		Colchester Borough Council
M S W Pearson	Leicester's Trams in Retrospect	The Tramway Museum Society.
R Markham	Public Transport in Ipswich	Ipswich Information Office
Stephen Cobb	Ipswich Buses An Illustrated History	Ipswich Buses Ltd
The Norwich Tramways 1900–1935		Tramway & Omnibus Historical Society.
Frank D Simpson	The Wolverton & Stony Stratford Steam Trams	Omnibus Society
G D Austin	Peterborough Tramways	Greater Peterborough Arts Council
S L Swingle	Cambridge Street Tramways	The Oakwood Press
W H Lucas	Memories of Grimsby and Cleethorpes Transport	Turntable Publications
W H Bett and J C Gillham (edited by J H Price)	The Tramways of the East Midlands and The Tramways of South Yorkshire and Humberside and The Tramways of the North Midlands	Railway and Transport League

In addition to the above, various copies of *Modern Tramway* (Ian Allan Ltd issued jointly with the Light Rail Transit Association), *SuperTram* (Ian Allan Ltd), *Tramway Review* (the historical journal of the LRTA) and *Tramfare* (the Tramway & Light Railway Society bulletin) were consulted.

Index